W9-BDS-431

Roll Call for Reform

Working Toward Making a Difference in Schools

Amanda M. Rudolph

ROWMAN & LITTLEFIELD EDUCATION
A division of
ROWMAN & LITTLEFIELD PUBLISHERS, INC.
Lanham • New York • Toronto • Plymouth, UK

Published by Rowman & Littlefield Education
A division of Rowman & Littlefield Publishers, Inc.
A wholly owned subsidiary of The Rowman & Littlefield Publishing Group, Inc.
4501 Forbes Boulevard, Suite 200, Lanham, Maryland 20706
www.rowman.com

10 Thornbury Road, Plymouth PL6 7PP, United Kingdom

British Library Cataloguing in Publication Information Available

Library of Congress Cataloging-in-Publication Data

Library of Congress Cataloging-in-Publication Data Available
ISBN 978-1-61048-065-9 (cloth : alk. paper) -- ISBN 978-1-61048-066-6 (pbk. : alk. paper) -- ISBN 978-1-61048-067-3 (electronic)

The paper used in this publication meets the minimum requirements of American National Standard for Information Sciences Permanence of Paper for Printed Library Materials, ANSI/NISO Z39.48-1992.

Printed in the United States of America

For Aubrey
Who changes the world everyday

Contents

Foreword

The past ten years have seen an incredible amount of change in the education policy world. In the past, the stereotypical teacher could just close the classroom door and theoretically teach the way he or she wanted to teach. But now, external accountability pressures have reached their long arm into the average classroom to fundamentally change the teaching profession. Twelve years after the passage of the No Child Left Behind Act of 2001 (NCLB), with new student assessments, the beginnings of an almost national Common Core curriculum, and changing teacher evaluations based in large part on student test scores, the eye of the political storm of change has now been turned on teacher educators—whether they like it or not. How are faculty prepared to deal with these changes, and how are they going to prepare future teachers to be prepared for the reality of today's classrooms?

How did the teacher accountability model make it to higher education? The logic model plays out in the following way. As NCLB passed in 2001, policy makers watched the US students' falling test scores on international benchmark tests and asked, *What is wrong with our students that they aren't competing well with other countries?* The policy answer was to create benchmarked achievement tests to determine where and how students were failing in their schooling and then have schools publicly report scores so that everyone could see how well schools were or were not doing. The average classroom teacher began to spend more and more time teaching to achievement tests and focusing on students passing these tests.

As some of these student testing results began to emerge, policy makers then began to ask, *What's wrong with our teachers that American children are not performing at the levels they should be?* Intense criticism of the teacher evaluation system swept through policy circles and resulted in policy requirements in the Race to the Top (RTTT) and American Recovery and

Reinvestment Act (ARRA) that required states to upend how they evaluated teachers. Cash-strapped states rushed to make changes to state policy in line with RTTT guidelines so that they, too, might have a slice of the competitive pie. Ten states ultimately received RTTT money, but over half of all states actually changed state policy in the hope that they might be awarded some of this money . . . and when they didn't receive any money, states then had a legislative mandate for often quick change to their teacher accountability system. The average classroom teacher, who already had some school pressure to make sure students did well on these high-stakes assessments to meet adequate yearly progress goals, now depended on students succeeding on these tests for their own increased compensation, tenure, and contract renewal. Most teachers did not have a problem with being assessed and receiving feedback on their teaching, but the measurements used to assess teacher performance (e.g., value-added scores) have often been criticized for their imprecise results and unfair application across schools.

As a condition of the acceptance of the RTTT money, states agreed to change how they measured the quality of their teacher preparation programs. With this shift in teacher education policy attention, in the past couple of years, the quality of teacher education has risen as a top issue for policy makers. *If students aren't performing well on international assessments, and US teachers are substandard and unable to teach our students, then what's wrong with the programs that are preparing teachers?* Consequently, teacher education is now at the center of the teacher quality policy conversation.

In the past two years, a series of reports and policies has been proposed and released that highlight these issues:

- The National Council for the Accreditation of Teacher Education (NCATE) released the Blue Ribbon Panel report (2010) that called for an increased emphasis on the clinical preparation of teachers. Authors of the report stated that teacher preparation needed to be "turned upside down."
- Stanford University, American Association of Colleges of Teacher Education (AACTE), and the Council of Chief State School Officers (CCSSO) began work on a national campaign for institutions of higher education (IHE) to implement a preservice, subject-specific performance assessment called the teacher performance assessment (edTPA).
- The US Department of Education (USDE) released a report titled *Our Future, Our Teachers* (2011)—USDE's first real focus on teacher preparation in its thirty-year history.
- In 2010, the National Council on Teacher Quality (NCTQ) and *U.S. News &World Report* announced that they would be completing a review of teacher preparation for publication. The announcement caused a heated debate between some teacher preparation providers and other stakeholders due to the nature of how programs would be reviewed.

- During Elementary and Secondary Education Act (ESEA) reauthorization debates in the fall of 2011 and 2012, both the House and the Senate included provisions focused on changing and improving the quality of teacher preparation.
- In 2010, NCATE and the Teacher Education Accreditation Council (TEAC) began negotiations to combine teacher education's two accreditations entities into one agency titled the Council for the Accreditation of Educator Preparation (CAEP). The revised CAEP accreditation standards are expected to be released for public comment in February 2013.
- In 2012, the USDE established the Negotiated Rulemaking panel for Title II of the Higher Education Act. The panel met for three sessions of two and a half days each through the winter and spring of 2012 but were unable to come to a consensus on rules. The USDE, therefore, will be making its own recommendations.
- CCSSO's new president, Commissioner Tom Luna of Idaho, announced that the focus of his term would be on creating a common standard for classroom readiness across the states.

Prior to 2010, teacher preparation had received little attention by policy makers or policy groups in Washington, DC. But, as is demonstrated above, the changing of teacher education is at the forefront of teacher quality policy debates.

Just like teachers at the beginning of NCLB, the teacher preparation community is at a precipice. At the turn of the twenty-first century, teachers and the organizations that represent them chose to fight any conversation about the use of standardized tests in determining teaching and teacher quality as well as conversations about how teacher accountability might be measured. Rather than recognizing that changes did need to be made and working with other stakeholders to identify measures that made sense, the teachers chose not to participate but instead to block reforms. Consequently, many decisions were made without teachers at the table.

Teacher preparation programs, especially college- and university-based programs, are now in a similar situation. Higher education faculty members and the organizations that represent them claim that teacher preparation is not as "bad" as policy makers and others claim them to be. However, higher education does not have the measures to show the impact of its teacher graduates in schools and classrooms. The edTPA is a good, national first step in this work, but many higher education faculty and organizations are not on board.

Dr. Rudolph's book is timely in our current political environment as it begins to challenge how current teacher education faculty prepare teachers for today's political context. In this new education world, teachers must be prepared for the realities of their chosen profession. Very rarely can they just go into a school, close their classroom doors, and still do whatever part of the curriculum they like the best. This book considers how faculty, practicing teachers, principals, districts, and teacher candidates must work together to ensure students are learning.

—Ann Nutter Coffman

Ann Nutter Coffman is a senior policy analyst. She served as a middle school teacher in West Virginia and Virginia as well as a district-based mentor and professional developer in Maryland before serving as a project director of a university-based teacher preparation program. Dr. Coffman's research and career has focused on issues of teacher preparation, policy implementation, school districts, and teacher quality. She earned a PhD from the University of Maryland and her MA and BA from West Virginia University.

Preface

In February of 2007 I sat in the audience at the Association of Teacher Educators annual conference in San Diego to hear Arthur Levine speak. Dr. Levine had recently published *Educating School Teachers* (2006), which criticized the teacher education programs in the United States. The mood of the room was somewhat tense, and although the platform for the speaker was centered in the ballroom, the majority of the audience was seated close to the doors. My colleagues and I chose a table a few rows back but directly in front of Dr. Levine. I had no idea what to expect from his speech, but he was engaging and concise.

After he had made a few points, he opened the floor to questions. Totally out of character, I raised my hand and reached for the cordless microphone. Here was my question: "I am a tenure-track assistant professor at a regional comprehensive university. I have been charged with revising our undergraduate teacher education program. I agree with some of what you said about teacher preparation. How am I supposed to make significant changes based on my current position?" And his answer surprised me.

He basically asked me if there was anyone else to lead the revisions. No. If I was getting compensated or release time to make these changes. No. Or if I had a good support system. Not really. His bottom line was that it was unfair to ask a junior faculty member to undertake such a large challenge. And then there were other questions.

I was not completely satisfied with his response, so at the encouragement of my colleague I approached Dr. Levine after the session. We talked for maybe five minutes, but what I said to him became very important to me. As we talked about education and teacher preparation, I said that as an assistant professor I feel impotent to make any significant or enduring change to teacher education. This idea was not something I had been thinking about or wrestling with, but it surfaced during that brief exchange. I thanked Dr. Levine for his time and comments. The next day I attended some sessions at the conference and headed home.

Upon my return to the university, I sought out my mentor, and we talked about my experiences at the conference and why they may be significant. It was during that conversation that I began to think about this book. If I felt impotent to make changes, then other university professors had to feel the same way. Over the next year I continued to reflect on this idea and address it with many of my students. The result is this book.

STATE OF EDUCATIONAL REFORM

Discussions of the state of education are rampant in the United States. The political arena is rife with positions and platforms for educational reform. President George W. Bush made education one of his major concerns as he promoted No Child Left Behind in 2001. The 2008 presidential race also included discussions of the state of education by all major candidates. The citizenry of the United States is aware of educational issues. Not only are politicians voicing criticisms of education, but so are major media leaders, including the *New York Times* and other publications.

In addition, leading business moguls like Bill Gates are taking a stance in education and offering solutions and incentives connected to monetary grants. For years university scholars have discussed and expounded on the need for systemic educational reform. Sarason (1996) and Fullan (1991) both state that systemic education change is needed in the United States and cannot be accomplished without the needed monetary, physical, and mental support. Sergiovanni (1994) and Barth (1990) also support educational reform and state that the key is a developed sense of community between the schools, teachers, and parents. However, in all of these different perspectives, one is unheard.

The voice of the classroom teacher is not as loud as the other voices of educational reform are. Where are the classroom teachers? Why are they not being heard? Who will speak for them? The current issues that face the classroom teacher range from overcrowding, highly diverse student populations and high-stakes testing and accountability to teacher evaluation, teacher isolation and attrition, low pay, lack of time, and on and on. Coping with the act of teaching on a daily basis leaves little time for teachers to become champions of systemic educational reform. To truly achieve a better educational environment for all students, teachers must be empowered and included in the reform process.

MY PERSONAL PERSPECTIVE

I have said repeatedly that I left the public school classroom so that I could make a difference in more students' lives. I want to make a difference in education. I thought I could make changes that others could not. I could make the changes that would allow all children to learn and grow.

I was prepared through a five-year MAT program with a thirty-week clinical experience. I graduated from a highly regarded Holmes partner program, and still I did not make it five years in the classroom. I tried to make changes in the public schools as a drama teacher and spent my time fighting bureaucratic issues like where to hold rehearsals. The reason I had become a teacher was to see the creativity in young children, but all I was doing was fighting about space and resources.

I tried to work in my field as a professional stage manager and was called back to education. I enrolled in a doctoral program in curriculum and instruction with an emphasis in arts education. I was sure this was the way to prepare myself to make some change to the educational system. If I taught 150 students as a high school teacher, I could reach thirty times as many in one class of future teachers.

I had two great mentors. One mentor supported me by offering continued support and encouragement. He was an advocate and still is for the students he guides. The other man challenged every thought I had about education. As we talked and read and read and talked, I realized that not many people I knew were really thinking critically about education.

I began to think about education in a different way. Why were we adhering to traditions based on past experiences? What about year-round schooling? Why do we still track students? What about grade levels? And on and on. It was a great time for me. My professors and peers had intellectual debates and discussion. I reveled in it. Then I graduated.

I taught as an adjunct for a year. It was like being in the Siberia of academia. I applied for jobs that year and was hired by a regional university two weeks before school started. Now I believed I would fit right into the faculty and begin to make the world better through education.

Immediately I realized something was amiss. My colleagues were not collaborative. They were not creative and innovative. They were not changing the world. In fact, most of them were trying to keep their own world afloat. The faculty members were busy with their own courses, with juggling the pressures of publishing and scholarship, with playing out the political chess game that comes with higher education. It was no fault of their own that they weren't changing the world. I could see that very quickly I, too, would be drowning in my own small pool of higher education.

So why was I prepared to be a change agent for the betterment of education when, in fact, I was going to be expected to teach overloads, run meetings, make presentations, and write papers? How was this helping anyone? What am I doing? And what is stopping me from changing the world?

In this book, I hope to address all these different challenges that faced me in different stages of my career. As I have thought more about change, I've realized I cannot do it alone and that helping me change the world is a responsibility of all these professional perspectives.

REFERENCES

Barth, R. S. (1990). *Improving schools from within.* San Francisco: Jossey-Bass.

Fullan, M. G. (1991). *The new meaning of educational change.* New York: Teachers College Press.

Levine, A. (2006). *Educating school teachers.* Washington, DC: The Education Schools Project.

Sarason, S. B. (1996). *Revisiting the culture of the school and the problem of change.* New York: Teachers College Press.

Sergiovanni, T. J. (1994). *Building community in schools.* San Francisco: Jossey-Bass.

Introduction

This book is intended to cross the experiences of many educators that work in teacher education. In order for educational reform to occur, all the stakeholders and leaders need to be present and held accountable. Many times educational reform is focused on a specific level or area; the need for all parties to work together is the key for successful change. Hopefully, this book addresses the different stakeholders and players in educational reform.

The purpose of this book is to explore the ideas of educational reform through public school, college, and university experiences as well as student and teacher experiences. The chapters in *Roll Call for Reform* address the specific issues for public school teachers and university professors in relation to educational reform. The major purpose of the book is to explore the parallel issues for public school and higher education teachers as well as the different challenges they both face as they work toward systemic school change.

There is a reason educational reform has not been successful in American education. The major reason is the disconnection between the university and the public school classroom. This missing link is a major detriment to the success of educational reform in the United States. University faculty are writing and researching many aspects of the change process and areas of educational change. However, little of that trickles down to the actual classroom teacher.

In addition, the traditions of teacher education are continually being supported and upheld. Innovative and unique approaches to teacher education that would facilitate educational change are few and far between in colleges and universities. To add to the problems, the university faculty are facing some of the same problems as the classroom teachers, including lack of time, overwhelming schedules, and lack of empowerment. Too often the higher

1

education arena is viewed as a business that must finally answer to the dollar. If there is no reform in higher education, in teacher education, then it will be almost impossible to sustain change in the public school. The two institutions are intimately connected, and, ultimately, educational reform will need to be sustained in higher education in order to support systemic reform of the PK–12 schools.

This book offers insight into the interwoven relationships between public schools and higher education institutions. By looking at the issues of educational reform from the perspectives of the classroom teacher and the university professor, the book offers a critical analysis of the challenges facing the United States in educational reform.

RATIONALE FOR PERSONAL PERSPECTIVE

Roll Call for Reform looks to make the change process relevant to individuals in every stage of education. Fullan (1991) states that no innovation will be completely implemented until the individual makes sense of the process. The individual must have ownership of the change in order for it to be sustained. Politicians can make laws, and principals can make unilateral adoptions of new methods. However, until the individual takes ownership, the change will be superficial. In order to understand how the individual feels and thinks about the change process in the different stages of her career, the book is written from varying perspectives. Hopefully, this approach will begin a discussion about empowerment and collaboration needed to make the changes in schools to help the children.

STRUCTURE OF THE BOOK

The book is divided into chapters focusing on each perspective. Each chapter begins with a narrative depicting experiences of each of the perspectives, including new teachers, adjunct faculty, and tenured university faculty. These narratives are based on some personal experiences, experiences of colleagues, and common issues that each teacher encounters. These narratives can be used as case studies for teacher education programs, including doctoral and leadership programs, or with classroom teachers in the PK–12 setting. The narratives are meant to paint a picture of how policy, change, and teacher preparation interact in an authentic environment. These narratives also address the challenges and strengths of each of the perspectives.

The chapters then focus on the obstacles specific to a particular perspective. Drawing on research, I discuss the obstacle facing educators. Each of these obstacles is discussed in detail in relation to that specific group. The strengths that each unique perspective brings to educational reform are also addressed. It is important to remember that although some roles and groups have more experience with change or time in the system, all perspectives have valuable strengths that are most likely not being utilized to make change.

The final section of each chapter is a call to action. In this section, ways to increase and utilize the strengths of each perspective are discussed. How can each group be empowered to use its unique strengths to improve the educational system in the United States? Additionally, there are suggestions for overcoming the obstacles to change for that particular group.

The final chapter of the book brings together the common ideas from the previous chapters to outline a call to action for educational reform of our system in the United States. The ideas presented cut across the perspectives and responsibilities of each group. By thinking about and trying out some collaborative and different approaches to change, we may actually improve education for all.

REFERENCE

Fullan, M. G. (1991). *The new meaning of educational change.* New York: Teachers College Press.

Chapter One

Teacher Preparation

Educator preparation programs are not the beginning of the preparation process for our future teachers. Our future teachers begin to develop ideas and perspectives on education from the moment they enter the school system, be it public or private. However, in this cycle of preparation, the educator preparation programs are a critical component, especially to transition our candidate from thinking as a student to thinking as a teacher. Part of that transition must be to also begin to think like an educational reformer.

In this chapter, perspectives related to the educator preparation process will be discussed. Teacher candidates face many issues as they matriculate through an educator preparation program. These issues vary, as do all educator programs. The narratives in this chapter deal with the different approaches to educator preparation. From this perspective, the obstacles and strengths of each will be discussed, with a final section offering direction for this perspective.

NARRATIVE

I Am Not Alone

Ms. McIver sat at the desk, tapping her pen and listening to her stomach rumble. It was 7:50 a.m. She had eaten a Pop-Tart for breakfast but was still hungry. Her supervising teacher from the university should be here in the next five minutes. He was coming to watch her first lesson during her internship year.

She was teaching a lesson on persuasive speaking to her first-period class. She had really never felt so alone. Was the lesson okay? Had she thought of everything? How could she even know? She really could not believe she was

6 Chapter 1

this nervous. After all, she knew Dr. Peters from previous classes. To calm her nerves, she decided to look at her lesson one more time.

"Hi, Ms. McIver," Dr. Peters said as he knocked on the door.

Ms. McIver got up and wiped her sweaty hands on her skirt before she shook his hand. "Hi. I'm a little nervous today."

"Don't worry. It will all go swimmingly. So we have ten minutes before class. Tell me what you are going to do. Also let me know what you think is going to work and what you might be worried about," Dr. Peters said.

"Okay. Let's see. I am going to present a lesson on persuasive speaking. The kids are going to have to take notes. I am not sure how that will go, but then they get to work in groups to create a persuasive ad for a product or service. I am pretty excited about that part of the lesson," Ms. McIver said in one breath.

Dr. Peters chuckled. "Okay then. Where would you like me to sit?"

"Oh, you can sit here at my desk. I will be up front," Ms. McIver said as the bell rang. Suddenly the halls filled with students and voices and laughter. As Ms. McIver gathered her materials and moved to the front of the class-room, students began streaming into the class. Ms. McIver took a deep breath and began welcoming each student with a smile, and Dr. Peters began taking notes.

Fifty minutes later, Ms. McIver looked up and realized class was over. The bell rang and the students left hurriedly. She walked to the back of the class to Dr. Peters.

"Now this is your conference period, right?" Dr. Peters asked.

"Right. You said to schedule our observation before our conference so we could immediately debrief," Ms. McIver answered.

"Let's get to it. First, I want you to tell me what you thought you did well. What really worked in this lesson?" Dr. Peters prompted.

"Well, I think the group work was good. I could have done better in the directions, but I really think they enjoyed working together, and I was pleased with their progress. We are going to continue working on the ads tomorrow," Ms. McIver said.

"Great. How do you think you could have improved the directions?" Dr. Peters asked.

Ms. McIver and Dr. Peters continued talking for forty-five minutes, shar-ing ideas, brainstorming ways to improve the lesson, and identifying the strengths and weaknesses of Ms. McIver.

"I would really like you to share the results of your small group work this evening in class. Would that be all right with you?" Dr. Peters asked.

"Sure. That sounds great," Ms. McIver said. She said good-bye to Dr. Peters and readied herself for the next five classes.

After school Ms. McIver went downstairs to the English classroom where she would have class with the other fifteen interns and Dr. Peters. She walked in with her stack of papers and her textbooks and looked around. Two math interns were coming in talking rapidly. Another intern from Spanish had already staked out some space. The desks were arranged in a circle, and a few were still open. She walked to a spot by Aubrey and took a seat.

"Hey, Aubrey. How's it going?" Ms. McIver said.

"Well, I am really not sure. I do know that I made it through the day," Aubrey said with a laugh.

Ms. McIver realized that no matter what this internship experience held for her, she was in it with fifteen other teachers and Dr. Peters. She was not alone.

NARRATIVE

This Is It?

Mr. Fields was checking his e-mail once again. School would start in fifteen minutes, and he was supposed to be observed this morning. He sent his supervising teacher an e-mail a week ago scheduling this observation. He was required to be observed three times during student teaching, and this was to be his second time. The first observation went fine, and his supervising teacher was very kind. This time was not going the same way.

Frustrated, Mr. Fields took out his cell phone to call his supervising teacher. It was five minutes to the bell. Just as he was about to click the Send button, Mrs. Popper walked in the door with her gray hair and warm cardigan. She was the epitome of the retired high school teacher.

"Good morning, Mr. Fields. I am right on time. I will get settled while you get ready," Mrs. Popper said as she pulled out her notepad and glasses.

"I wasn't sure you were coming this morning. Do we need to talk about my lesson first?" Mr. Fields asked.

"Oh, heavens no. I have seen so many social studies lessons I could do this with my eyes closed," Mrs. Popper said.

Great, thought Mr. Fields as he turned on the computer and projector. As he got the classroom ready, he wondered why he even had a supervising teacher. His cooperating teacher at the school was more helpful and interested in what he was doing. This supervisor from the college only seemed to want to get a check. What made it all the worse was that he really wanted some input and feedback about what he was doing in the class.

"Mrs. Popper, could you give me some feedback on my PowerPoint today? We are studying the branches of the government and I want to make sure the students understand," Mr. Fields asked.

"Oh my. I really don't know anything about that technology stuff," Mrs. Popper giggled. "Just do your best, dear."

At that moment, Mr. Fields felt a little lost, but he could not dwell on it because the bell rang and the students came flooding in. Soon everyone was seated, and Mr. Fields put on a smile and began to discuss the legislative branch of government.

As the class finished and the students began leaving, Mr. Fields saw Mrs. Popper gathering her things and walking to the door. He tried to disengage himself from the barrage of questions from students, but he was too late. She was out the door.

He finally made it over to his desk. There, in the middle of the desk, was a single sheet of carbon paper. He counted five checkmarks in the exceptional category. There were also two comments. "Well done," and "Great enthusiasm."

Mr. Fields sat down at the desk and put his head in his hands. He felt lost and alone. He did not know how to make the connections between what he learned in college and what he was doing now. Where were his professors? Why was a retired teacher supervising him? How was he going to make it for ten more weeks?

After a minute, Mr. Fields picked up his head and looked at the evaluation again. He did not know what he was going to do, but he did know it was all up to him.

OBSTACLES TO EDUCATIONAL REFORM

This perspective faces several obstacles to educational reform. The preservice teacher must progress through an immense curriculum in a short amount of time and then make the connections between theory and practice in a clinical setting. The new era of accountability in teacher education limits the focus of the curriculum to leave out the role of change agent for preservice teachers. Finally, the preservice curriculum can be disconnected from schools, insulated in the world of academia.

Curriculum and Clinical Practice

Traditional teacher education curriculum is divided into a few main categories. Most teacher preparation programs have classes in instructional methods, assessment, classroom management, diversity, and possibly technology. Within each of these areas the amount of knowledge needed to be an effective teacher is immense. Learning about instructional methods should include general methods, pedagogical content knowledge, differentiation of instruction, and more. One three-hour class cannot cover all that is needed for effective teaching.

In addition, the preservice teachers are typically learning about instruction and assessment and classroom management in a university classroom setting. Many classes are still held on university campuses with little connection to real PK–12 classroom settings. Research supports that modeling is one of the most effective ways to teach (Bandura, 1986). Yet we are teaching future teachers to teach in an inauthentic environment. The teacher candidates need to be able to apply what they are learning in an authentic learning environment, a classroom with PK–12 students. This implies that the traditional teacher education program would need to implement earlier and more meaningful field experiences and integrate the classroom teacher.

The issues continue at the student teaching stage of preparation. Obviously, there are outstanding programs that require extensive clinical practice. There are residency master of arts in teaching programs that are developed as five-year programs that culminate with a year-long internship. However, these are not the typical programs for the majority of teacher preparation programs. Twelve- to sixteen-week student teaching programs are still the majority. Again, these programs can be highly effective, but the key is continuity of the curriculum and continued support of the faculty and involvement of the practitioners.

Disconnection from Schools

This perspective can also be challenged by the disconnection between universities and schools. As discussed previously, the student teaching experience and previous field experience may offer only a glimpse into the realities of the American public school. Not only do the preservice teachers need connection to the public schools, but their professors also need that connection. Many teacher educators begin their careers in the public school classroom, but as their higher education career progresses, the experiences they had as a public school teacher become outdated. Professors need to keep a connection to public schools in order to hear and see firsthand the changes in students and changes facing teachers.

The movement toward professional development schools (PDS) years ago created partnerships for teacher education and public schools. Many of these PDS partnerships are still working today. However, many of the teacher education programs that began working as PDS models have drifted away from the philosophy and intent of the original charter. Turnover in administration in both higher education and the school districts as well as turnover in faculty have led to a watered-down version of a PDS.

Many times the incentives for partnering have disappeared and the importance of working together has been replaced with large amounts of work toward accountability. These PDS programs may still be operating but are more likely to be about placements and numbers of students than professional development. In essence, the university and the school may have a relationship, but they are still disconnected on the issues facing both institutions.

Accountability

The American public school system has been operating under a system of accountability for some time now. No Child Left Behind (NCLB) made sure all states had high-stakes testing in place and that teachers were held accountable. Whether this system is effective or not is not the question for this discussion. The fact is that all states are holding public schools accountable by standardized testing systems. In some cases, the pressures of such high-stakes accountability systems have led to more constrictive and controlled curriculum and instruction in school districts.

In order to make sure the students pass the standardized tests and benchmarks, administrators and teachers emphasize the testing format and single concepts that will be included. The integration of assessment with curriculum and instruction is not looked at as an option for preparing students to pass the benchmark measure. This narrow focus on assessment leads to a divisive environment between universities and schools.

Universities encourage student teachers to try various methods and instructional strategies at the same time as districts are narrowing their focus and instruction. The current systems of school district accountability and the curriculum of the teacher education programs are out of line, even so much that some classroom teachers decline student teachers because the process may interfere with the scores on the accountability measures.

STRENGTHS OF THIS PERSPECTIVE

Interestingly, there are some important strengths to this perspective. The university setting has a long history of leading ideas in many disciplines. It can still be that for teacher education. Secondly, there is a wide variety of teacher preparation programs that meet the needs of diverse learners today. Also, the preservice teacher has the ability to make a direct impact on the learning in PK–12 settings.

Strengths of the Academy

One of the major strengths of this perspective is the tradition of the academy. Institutions of higher education can offer preservice teachers training with cutting-edge instructions and methods. Faculty members at universities are constantly conducting research into best practices and current issues facing education in the United States. In addition, higher education has access to millions of dollars in grant monies. Programs in educator preparation can fund program evaluation and changes through grant money. Many times grants will fund curricular development and professional development related to a specific need or issue in education. In this sense, university-based educator preparation programs can provide up-to-date instructional methods and approaches for the preservice teacher.

The depth of a teacher education curriculum can also offer preservice teachers a foundation of knowledge in change and the change process. Undergraduate preservice teachers can learn that the profession requires them to become change agents and advocates of growth in the field. Professors can mentor and support undergraduates in action research and policy investigations. Preservice teachers can be given the tools to work toward educational reform.

Variety of Education Preparation Approaches

Another strength of the preservice teacher perspective is the different approaches to preparing and training preservice teachers. Today's preservice teachers are being prepared in variety of environments. This diversity of experience can provide the future teachers with a wide variety of perspectives and opportunities. The responsibility for education comes down to the community desires and needs. In order to make changes and create opportunities for growth, the teacher workforce needs to be comprised of new teachers with a broad spectrum of experience and perspective.

Within the scope of the traditional undergraduate preparation programs, preservice teachers are completing coursework in their content areas as well as in educational theory and practice. They are completing clinical and field experiences ranging from twelve weeks to a full school year. In alternative programs, preservice teachers are spending time in classrooms under the guidance of a supervising teacher, gaining hands-on experience. Arguments rage over the best approach to teacher preparation, but for the sake of improving the system, the current variety of approaches lends a broad view of students and schools for our preservice teacher candidates.

Impact of Teacher Candidates on PK–12 Students

The National Council for Accreditation of Teacher Education (NCATE) and the new accrediting body, the Council for the Accreditation of Educator Preparation (CAEP), both stress the importance of the impact of teacher education candidates on PK–12 students (NCATE, 2008). NCATE accredited schools have been documenting the impact of their candidates on PK–12 students for some time. This is sometimes a challenge to document, but NCATE believes that the preservice teacher can and should make a positive impact on the PK–12 students. This potential for achievement and growth is the most critical benefit of this perspective for initiating change.

While involved in clinical and field experiences, preservice teachers can be afforded the freedom and time to spend with small groups of students and individual students. Individual and small group instruction can be effective in increasing achievement of students. In addition, these preservice teachers can also be empowered to implement new strategies and practices learned in their preparation programs. The preservice teacher can also be a resource for the supervising teacher for new materials and practices or act as a liaison to the university for professional development. Many times the clinical practices component of teacher preparation is not as connected to the momentum of the university as the preparation courses are. Teacher preparation programs need to think of ways to utilize the preservice teacher in ways that work toward reform and revitalizing the profession.

MOVING FORWARD

To engage preservice teachers in a conversation about change and educational reform, universities need to make an effort to specifically address the issues. To help grow change agents, we need to keep high standards for teacher education programs. Universities should increase the clinical experiences for the preservice teacher and continue a connection to faculty and teachers during those experiences.

High Standards for Teacher Education Programs

NCATE commissioned the Blue Ribbon Panel to recommend a direction for teacher preparation programs in the United States. In 2010, *Transforming Teacher Education through Clinical Practice: A National Strategy to Prepare Effective Teachers* was released, calling for higher standards in teacher preparation (NCATE, 2010). Among the recommendations were more rigorous accountability, strengthening candidate selection and placement, revamping curricula, incentives, and staffing, supporting partnerships, and expanding the knowledge base to identify what works and supports continuous improvement (2010).

These recommendations are not surprising or radical. Teacher education has been referred to as the backup plan for students and the default major for "those who can't" for years. It is time to seriously and uniformly implement high standards for the education profession. However, this cannot be accomplished just by higher education institutions. Public schools are critical in deciding student placements, developing curricula, working as partners, and identifying what works.

Schools and universities need to recruit the brightest and most eager students into the profession of education. Secondary students need to see the education profession as a viable career choice, not just a fallback. If change is going to happen, the profession will need educators who are devoted to their career, not just there to have summers off. In order to have serious, dedicated educators, there must be high standards in place for the preservice teachers and the teacher preparation programs.

More Clinical Practice

Only so much can be learned from a course in education; preservice teachers need an opportunity to apply what they learn. Most, if not all, teacher education programs require some form of clinical practice. However, these experiences vary across the country. Even within a program, two preservice teachers in clinical experiences may come away with completely different perspectives of education and the classrooms in the United States. An effort to standardize the clinical practice is needed.

For years, teacher preparation has been compared with the medical preparation model. How are they similar? Why is medical preparation so much longer? What can we learn from the successes of medical schools? Obviously, the medical student and the preservice teacher are two different cases, but teacher education can make some connections. The medical student is supervised for an extended period of time in many different settings by trained mentors. The preservice teacher will be responsible for a nine-month school year and yet will practice for only twelve weeks. The new teacher is certified to teach his content area and grade level in any school in the state; yet each school district and campus is varied, with different percentages of students with low socioeconomic status, English language learners, at-risk students, migrant families, and races. An extended clinical practice would allow for the preservice teacher to experience and practice in a variety of settings. Practicing the profession with multiple populations would enhance the knowledge base and increase the skills of the preservice teachers.

An additional benefit to extended clinical practice is the support the preservice teacher receives from his mentor. A longer experience allows the young teacher and the veteran teacher to work together as peers and develop a relationship that is based on trust in the classroom. This professional relationship supports the efforts of the preservice teacher in attempting new approaches to instruction in a safe environment while also challenging the mentor teacher to open her classroom to new perspectives and people. By extending the clinical practice, relationships can be fostered that support the ideas of incorporating innovation and reformation into the classroom.

Continued Connection to Faculty

Again, there is a wide spectrum of experiences in the clinical practice phase of teacher preparation. In some cases, the candidate is fostered and mentored continuously by university faculty that he has had for coursework and classes prior to the fieldwork. However, in some, mostly larger, programs, the clinical practice is removed from the university faculty and assigned to adjunct faculty for supervision. By no means is this an indictment against adjunct faculty; the positive role of adjunct faculty in education is addressed later in the book. The issue with relying solely or mainly on adjunct faculty for supervision of preservice teachers is the disconnection to the university and at times the field sites.

Adjunct faculty members tend to be disconnected from the day-to-day world of the university. This means as supervisors they may not be aware of changes in teacher preparation curriculum, updates in practices, and changes in legislation that affect teacher preparation, schools, and teachers. It becomes the responsibility of the university to continually support and train these supervisors. If adjuncts are used for supervision, it is critical to maintain a connection to the university and the preservice teachers and the school district.

No matter who is supervising the preservice teacher in clinical practice, adjunct or tenure-track faculty, the preservice teacher needs to have a continued connection to the university faculty members. This relationship allows for candidates to revisit ideas and practices they were taught with the actual instructor. In essence, it is the final loop in the spiraling of the teacher education curriculum. The university faculty member also benefits by experiencing the happenings and events in the public schools serving as field sites.

This connection can enhance the instruction of the preservice courses; faculty members can make changes and additions based on what they are actually seeing in the public schools. An alignment between the field sites and the teacher preparation curriculum will better prepare the future classroom teacher. It also allows for a combined focus for changes within the schools. A public school wrestling with reading scores can lead to a stronger focus on reading strategies in the preservice curriculum, which will provide the district with better prepared teachers that are more effective in reading.

University faculty must maintain a continued presence in the clinical practice phase of educator preparation in order for the profession to grow.

CONCLUSIONS

Preservice teacher preparation offers unique challenges to educational reform. The pressures of accountability and the constraints placed on the education curriculum are significant hurdles for preparing preservice teachers to become change agents. On the other hand, this perspective has some powerful strengths, including the direct impact on PK–12 students. In order to take full advantage of this population, teacher educators must strive for high standards in preparation, enhance and expand clinical practice, and maintain connections to the clinical practice experience.

REFERENCES

Bandura, A. (1986). *Social foundations of thought and action: A social-cognitive theory.* Englewood Cliffs, NJ: Prentice-Hall.

National Council for Accreditation of Teacher Education. (2008). *Professional standards for the accreditation of teacher preparation institutions.* Washington, DC: Author.

National Council for Accreditation of Teacher Education. (2010). *Transforming teacher education through clinical practice: A national strategy to prepare effective teachers.* Washington, DC: Author.

Chapter Two

A New Teacher

As educators think about reform and change for the public school system, the perspective of the new teacher is increasingly important. This specific group bridges the gap between the preparation of teachers and the cadre of experienced veterans. Within this group lies a choice of paths—blazing a trail of change and innovation or taking the worn path to maintain the status quo. New teachers face a myriad of challenges in the first few years. Teacher attrition is highest in the first three to five years of teaching (Ingersoll, 2001). This stage of educator development and the challenges faced determine the future of the teacher. Will she stay or will she go?

In this chapter, the experiences related to the new teacher will be discussed. The narratives included in this chapter deal with the bureaucracy of the system and the issues related to restrictive curriculum. The chapter will also address the specific obstacles and strengths of new teachers. The final section will talk about where we as educators go from here.

NARRATIVE

The Power of the System

Ms. Landrum walked into her chemistry classroom early on Monday morning. It was still early in the first semester, and she could see the changing leaves through her classroom window. She felt comfortable as she threw her keys on the desk and sat down to review the week's lesson plans. Shipley High School was her second school in as many years.

Ms. Landrum graduated and took the only job she could find in an urban school district. She had always known she wanted to move back to her small hometown, so as soon as the position opened up in Shipley, she moved, although it was difficult to start at another school so quickly. Luckily, she had plenty of lesson plans and experiments accumulated from college and her first year of teaching. Last year had been challenging, and she was looking forward to an easier year at a more familiar and smaller school.

Ms. Landrum glanced at the clock on her computer. 7:23. She still had time to check her lab materials for the week before the bell rang to begin the day. Last week in the department meeting, the department chair, Mr. Fields, spoke at length again about the new curriculum and how important it was to follow the timeline.

Apparently, the district thought that adopting benchmark testing for each subject would help each school meet its goals for adequate yearly progress. So now each subject had to administer the same six-weeks test to all the classes. Ms. Landrum did not really mind. It kept her moving, and she thought the students were understanding the concepts.

Her students scored well on the first benchmark test, and the next one was coming up in two weeks. She knew there were a few concepts on it that she had not covered yet, but it would all come together with this week's lesson and experiment.

Ms. Landrum walked to the supply closet, her smart teacher shoes click-clacking as she went. Sometimes she really missed the flip-flop days of college. She grabbed a basket and started collecting supplies for the experiment. She had everything except sodium hydroxide and hydrochloric acid. She remembered ordering these before school started. After looking for unopened boxes and receipts for shipment, she decided to go ask the secretary in the front office.

As she entered the front office, she saw the secretary, Mrs. Hill, talking on the phone and looking at her computer screen. Ms. Landrum waited patiently for ten minutes. Then Mrs. Hill ended the phone call and noticed her.

"Oh, hi, dear. What can I do for you?" Mrs. Hill chirped.

"I was hoping you could help me. I am trying to prepare for an experiment this week, and I am out of two chemicals. I am pretty sure I ordered them before school started, but I can't seem to find them anywhere. Can you see if they have been shipped?" Ms. Landrum asked.

"Oh, sure. What was the PO number?" Mrs. Hill asked.

"I don't know . . . do I need that?" Ms. Landrum said.

"Not really. I can just look it up on the account. What is your account number?" Mrs. Hill asked.

"Oh, I don't have it with me. Do I need to run and get it?" Ms. Landrum asked.

"Well, do you know the date you ordered it? Or the company you ordered it from?" Mrs. Hill asked.

"I think it was from School Chemicals in August," Ms. Landrum said.

"Here it is. Hmm. Let's see. Well, you ordered some other supplies the week before and after that you were $2.12 short in your budget for the chemical order. That's why we didn't order it."

Ms. Landrum wasn't sure she had heard correctly. "It wasn't ordered?" Mrs. Hill shook her head.

"What am I supposed to do? The students have to do this lab in order to do well on the benchmark. I need those chemicals," Ms. Landrum said.

"Well, I suppose we could order it with fewer bottles. Would that work?" Mrs. Hill asked.

"Oh, I can do it with less. That would be great. When will it be here?" Ms. Landrum asked.

"It should only take three weeks," Mrs. Hill said.

Ms. Landrum took a deep breath and slowly left the office. She thought about how she had been so excited to be a teacher, how she had engaging lessons and new ideas, and how she felt lucky to work with kids and see them get it. Now she was part of a system, and the system had the power to affect and change her engaging lessons. No one had told her how to work in the system.

NARRATIVE

Whose Instruction?

The note on Mr. Bradley's door said "Please see me as soon as you can. Mr. Smith." As he read it, Mr. Bradley's stomach dropped. Mr. Smith was the principal of the elementary school, and in his three years here, Mr. Bradley had never been called to the office. In fact, Mr. Bradley had never been called to the office ever.

Mr. Bradley opened the door to his third-grade class, an action that never failed to cheer him up until today. As he arranged the chairs around the tables and set out new books in the literacy center, he struggled to come up with some reason for the summons. When he read the note he immediately assumed he was in trouble, but maybe it was something good. Maybe he was doing something right. He read the note again, and his stomach dropped again, and now his hands were sweating. Definitely bad news.

Mr. Bradley walked toward the front office with his lunch in his hand. As he approached the teacher's lounge where he intended to store his lunch in the cluttered refrigerator, he saw Mr. Smith coming out of the door.

"Mr. Bradley, do you have a minute? I'd like to talk to you. Come on down to my office," Mr. Smith said.

"Okay," Mr. Bradley said as he realized he really wasn't being given a choice. He glanced longingly at the refrigerator as the lounge door swung shut. He took his lunch with him as he followed Mr. Smith to his office. They walked right past the receptionist into Mr. Smith's office. The principal motioned for Mr. Bradley to take a seat across the desk from him. Mr. Bradley chose the seat closest to the desk and sat up straight with his brown paper bag in both hands in his lap.

Mr. Smith sat down with his hand folded on his desk. "How are things going with you this year?" he asked.

Mr. Bradley, still not knowing where this was going, replied, "Great, sir."

"Good, I'm glad. I was hoping we could talk about one thing today. Do you remember last week when Mrs. Carmichael did your walk-through evaluation?" Mr. Smith said.

"Of course. She came during math," Mr. Bradley said. He was in fact relieved; he knew he did a great job when the assistant principal had been there.

"That's what I want to talk about. Mrs. Carmichael was concerned because during the math lesson you used some strategies and activities that were not part of standardized curriculum for the district. Can you tell me about that?" Mr. Smith asked.

"Well, I know we are all supposed to use that one math program, but I have several students who just are not getting it. And last summer I attended a great workshop on manipulatives and English-language learners, and I thought I would give it a try. They really seemed to enjoy the activity. I think they got a lot out of it," Mr. Bradley said. He was happy to explain what he had been doing. It had been a success.

"I see. Mr. Bradley, I must say I am a little disappointed. I can understand where you may think you know best, but the district has put a great deal of time and money into our math program. We need everyone to adhere to the program. Do you understand?" Mr. Smith said.

"Not really. I am using the program. I just supplemented it. Is that wrong?" Mr. Bradley asked.

"In this district, you will teach the adopted program and that is all. There is no supplementing and no deviations. Is that clear?" Mr. Smith said in a more firm voice.

"Yes. That is clear." Mr. Bradley paused. There were so many things he wanted to say. So many reasons that Mr. Smith was wrong, so many ways to explain how the students got it, so many arguments for meeting the needs of all students. Then he looked back at Mr. Smith. His face was set and rigid. Mr. Bradley said, "Is that all?"

OBSTACLES TO EDUCATIONAL REFORM

The new teacher tends to be prepared for lesson planning and instruction but not prepared to act as a change agent in the public school system. Understandably, teacher education programs are taxed by the amount of content and coursework needed to prepare new teachers; reforming the system is a low priority in the curriculum when put up against high-stakes testing and accountability. However, there are other obstacles that prevent the new teacher from effecting change in the school system. The four main issues facing this group are lack of understanding in working in a bureaucracy, disconnection between new teachers, the new teacher identity, and scope of efficacy.

Working in a Bureaucracy

The new teacher is prepared with strategies for classroom management and instruction and assessment. Most programs even offer a field experience or student teaching experience to practice what they have learned. However, nowhere in the curriculum are they taught how to work in a bureaucracy. The new teacher faces the challenges of copiers, and budgets, and documentation, and procedures.

These administrative duties connected to the profession take some time to adjust to as a new teacher. In addition to planning instruction and assessments for each class taught, the new teacher must also consider the paper supply he is allotted for the year and how that may effect his future lessons. On a larger scale, new teachers must reconcile the instructional preparation they had in their postsecondary experience with the realities of the district curriculum in place, and if that does not happen, many new teachers lose their enthusiasm for teaching.

Curricular issues have become more prescriptive in recent years. As the system of accountability grows in the United States, the pressures on classroom teachers and school administrators increase. One response to the high-stakes testing in the United States is an attempt by school administrators to control for any variability in the classrooms by providing a set curriculum. Having district goals or standards is necessary for educating all students. We want all students to learn and grow. However, there is a fine line between a set of standards and a set method of instruction. New teachers face a culture of accountability and assessment that sometimes lends itself as an excuse for top-down decisions in classroom instruction.

The new teacher may be put in a situation where the curriculum and instructional approaches are outlined by the school. In a case like that, the new teacher must be able to critically evaluate the provided materials and make an informed decision. The decision may be to implement the provided curriculum, or it may be to supplement the curriculum with other resources and approaches. Or the evaluation may result in an opinion that the materials are insufficient. No matter what the outcome, the new teacher should be able to critically evaluate and then support that evaluation with a valid argument backed up by data and research. Unfortunately, at this time few new teachers are equipped with those skills when they begin in the schools.

Disconnection

During the teacher preparation programs, the new teachers were invested in courses and programs with other students. Classes were delivered to groups of soon-to-be teachers. Discussions ensued. Projects were created. Allies were made, and respect for differences was nurtured. Nowhere in this preparation experience was the new teacher left alone or cast adrift. The picture of the first-year classroom with a new teacher is drastically different.

In the first year, the new teacher is often disconnected. The initial preparations for the year are hurried and widespread. The new teacher readies her room. Acquires materials. Plans lessons and units. Often this work begins early in the morning and ends late in the night—at school and at home. This critical work is done solitarily; other new teachers are readying their own rooms and lessons. The feelings of safety created in a college experience are gone, and the teacher is alone.

The implications of this disconnection are directed not at effectiveness in teaching but at the effectiveness of reform. Teachers have worked in this disconnected way for decades, and there has been effective teaching from the model, but this model of disconnection may not lead to effective change in the school. New teachers are trying to survive the first few years of teaching, and little time is spent trying to effect change in the school, the district, or the system. Even if a new teacher wanted to begin to change the culture of the school, he would have to first make connections with other teachers. In the first few years of teaching there is little time to devote to building connections and forging a collaborative relationship.

New Teacher Identity

For argument's sake, let's say a new teacher has an idea for an innovation to make connections between parents and teachers of English-language learners. Not only would that teacher have to overcome the obstacles of the bureaucracy and the disconnections between teachers, but she would also have to overcome the stereotypes of a new teacher. Many times, new teachers are thought of by veteran teachers as inexperienced and idealistic. Very rarely are the new teachers seen as a resource for the programs or the schools in which they are working.

Many former students of mine have reported the veteran or mentor teachers they work with offer perspectives such as, "We tried that ten years ago and it didn't work then. When I close the door to my classroom, it is mine and I do what I want." Others offer advice, saying, "You think that now, but you'll learn." The idealism and fresh perspectives of the new teacher are not valued or called upon as resources for the schools. If the comments from the veteran teachers continue, the new teacher runs the risk of becoming jaded and withdrawn. If one hears things often enough, one comes to believe what he hears.

The identity of the new teacher and the perspectives she has to offer need to be channeled for positive use. The idealism can be focused on the individual classroom instead of the whole school. The inexperience can open new opportunities for the teachers to try new strategies or try old strategies in new ways. The focus on the classroom allows for growth of the new teacher and his sense of efficacy.

Efficacy

As we have discussed, the new teacher faces many challenges in her first classroom. In the first few years, the new teacher learns to navigate the bureaucracy of schools, learns to work in isolation or learns ways to overcome isolation and make connections, and also learns how to channel his energy into positive outlets. All of these experience lead to a greater sense of efficacy.

The new teacher is feeling competent and comfortable in the classroom after two or three years of teaching. Most teachers continue to feel more and more confident in their jobs after gaining classroom experience. This sense of efficacy is critical to the development of effective teachers. However, this sense of efficacy is usually limited to the classroom.

In teaching teachers who have returned for graduate degrees, I have heard many say that they feel comfortable teaching their students but could never teach their peers a new strategy or instructional method. These veteran teachers are lacking a sense of efficacy for the profession. They feel that they are effective with students but have little to offer the profession or their peers.

This is even more pronounced in new teachers. Instead of letting new teachers just survive the first few years, administrators and veteran teachers should help them establish an identity within the profession. Supporting new teachers by enabling them to join professional associations and attend professional development opportunities could go a long way toward helping the new teachers thrive as professionals. Only then can they gain the confidence necessary to try to implement changes and reforms in their schools.

STRENGTHS OF THIS PERSPECTIVE

Although new teachers face many challenges to becoming effective change agents, they do have some inherent strengths. New teachers should be looked on as resources for beginning change efforts within a district. This group brings to the system some unique perspectives and talents. These teachers are still developing their identity and have not lost a sense of idealism. These teachers are also coming out of preparation programs that are focusing on current trends and new strategies in education, and they also bring a desire for collaboration.

New Teacher Identity

Although I previously discussed new teacher identity as an obstacle, it can also be one of the strengths of this perspective. The idealism that the new teacher brings to the classroom and school can be contagious. As programs and departments grow and add newer teachers to the faculty, the fresh perspective and the energy of a new professional can reignite the passion in the veteran teachers on staff. Stable, well-established faculties with veteran teachers can use the energy and eagerness of the new teacher to begin conversations about curriculum and instruction.

The new teachers come to the school year with visions of engaging class lessons, active student learning, few discipline problems, and high achievement of students. These are the standards that the educator preparation programs have given them. They are ready, but sometimes the obstacles they face can make maintaining these standards difficult. Instead of leaving the new teacher on his own, the veteran teachers should help him focus his energies on effective instruction and guide the new teacher through the obstacles. And while they are working together, the veteran teachers can also learn from the eagerness of the new teacher to work toward educational reform.

Best Preparation

The new teacher also offers expertise to schools. Education preparation programs range from regional institutions to research universities, but the professors are current in research and new innovations in teacher education. In addition, the new teacher has been prepared by programs that are responding to the political movements in the United States. No Child Left Behind affected preparation programs, and movement toward Common Core standards and college readiness have also changed preparation programs. The new teachers are coming into school ready to hold all students to high expectations.

Changes in the demographics of the United States have made the need for effective teachers of English-language learners a critical need. More and more programs are including language acquisition and ELL instruction in their curriculum. The needs of the nation are changing the way teachers are prepared. These changes in teacher preparation are producing new teachers with cutting-edge strategies for instruction.

Although a great deal has been discussed in public in the past few years about teacher preparation and the state of our schools by the likes of Art Levine and the National Council on Teacher Quality, teacher preparation programs are still trying to produce the best teachers possible. The argument is not that teacher preparation programs are perfect and are perfectly preparing new teachers but that even though the preparation programs are challenged, they are still providing a better preparation for new teachers than many of the alternatives.

Collaborative

Teachers work in isolation (Goodlad, 1984). Teachers have an individual classroom and are responsible for specific students. However, that isolation takes a toll, including burnout (Schlichte, Yssel, & Merbler, 2005). Working together as professionals can have many benefits for the future of education.

The new teacher is looking for collaborative opportunities. She is not sure about the district curriculum or policies and looks for someone to help her navigate the process. By identifying a veteran teacher to help the new teacher, opportunities for collaboration abound. Collaboration does not mean that the teachers work on the same lessons and same instructional units or that they share a classroom or students. Collaboration in relation to reform means that the teachers are talking, discussing, sharing, and learning together as professionals. Having a new teacher who feels the need for guidance can open up the hallways for sharing among teachers.

The new teacher is comfortable sharing and discussing ideas since he is not too far removed from the higher education setting. He may casually start conversations about professional development opportunities in the district. These conversations can grow, and as more teachers participate, momentum builds that can be captured and focused toward educational reform.

MOVING FORWARD

As with all the perspectives presented in this book, the new teacher is a critical component to effecting change in schools. This group faces many challenges but also brings unique strengths to the school system. The questions are now: What can be done to help this group? How can new teachers be empowered? Three possible ways to give voice to new teachers are mentoring programs, quality field experiences, and school district input in preparation.

Mentoring Programs

Mentoring programs for new teachers is not a new idea. Most schools probably have a mentoring program in place for first-year teachers. This issue is
the quality and quantity of the mentoring. A principal is required to attend to
many different issues at one time while leading a school, and she cannot also
take on the oversight of a mentoring program. Typically, an administrator
may assign a formal mentor to a new teacher. This mentor may or may not
"click" with the new teacher, but given the time constraints and budget issues
facing administration, it is amazing that any mentor gets assigned.

Hopefully, the new teacher makes an effort to work with the assigned
mentor while also seeking an informal mentor. Prior to my first year of
teaching I was given the advice to find both a new teacher to get to know and
a veteran teacher to get to know. This is the advice I still give my students. It
made the challenges of my first year easier to handle with a sympathetic
friend and a knowledgeable colleague. Unfortunately, this advice puts the
burden of mentoring on the new teacher. How can we assure a supported,
meaningful mentoring experience the first year?

First, identify an invested leader for the mentoring program. This person
could be an administrator, a teacher, or even a staff member. But this person
needs to be dedicated to the program and an advocate for its continuation.
This leader can then spend time with the new teachers, getting to know them
early, and should also know the strengths of the veteran teachers on staff.
The mentor leader can then make more meaningful assignments or facilitate
the process of choosing mentors between new teachers and the veteran teachers.

Second, the mentors need mentoring. The mentor leader should meet with
the mentors regularly to debrief about the process and the evolution of the
mentoring relationship. The mentoring process does not need to be burdened
with "adminstrivia"; the process just needs to be attended to. The mentors
need a place to share their experiences and gain insight to the challenges
facing the new teachers in order to better serve the mentee they have.

The mentoring experience should be extended beyond the first year of
teaching. The profession loses so many teachers in the first few years that it
is critical to nurture and protect the new teachers as long as possible. As the
new teachers grow, the process of mentoring should become integrated into
their sense of the profession so that not only are we mentoring and supporting the new teacher in his development, but we are also growing future
mentors for future new teachers.

Finally, the university teacher preparation programs need to be involved
in the mentoring program. These professionals spend years with the teachers
they are preparing, only to sever the relationship upon graduation. These
professors are also stretched thin by the requirements of licensure and current

budget issues, but the connection to the students (new teachers) could be sustained. University programs could offer social networking sites and alumni opportunities for new teachers to connect not only to each other but also to the faculty.

Maintaining an e-mail database for graduates and sending newsletters with information regarding the profession could be helpful. The idea is not to have a formal, one-on-one mentoring program but rather an informal line of communication that is constant for the new teacher. Many times the university may be the point of communication of changes to the profession rather than the school district, and that should be reason enough to continue the conversation with graduates.

Clinical Practice and Field Experiences

Clinical practice and field experiences have been the focus of national discussion, both positive and negative, in the past few years (NCATE, 2010). Basically, what we know is that programs with extended field experiences prepare more effective teachers. The more teacher education candidates are in the schools, the more prepared they will be to be effective classroom leaders. In a perfect system, the candidates could do a year-long residency in a public school with a classroom teacher, district mentor, and university supervisor. Realistically, there are multiple issues surrounding a move to that type of program, including funding, time, personnel, and marketability to students.

Nevertheless, teacher preparation programs need to start thinking creatively to increase the length and quality of field experiences for their teacher candidates. Programs can integrate field experiences throughout coursework, requiring hours of experience in all education courses. Clinical placements could be created for coteaching models to build collaboration and collegiality among new teachers. Technology needs to be integrated so that student teachers and interns can debrief with faculty members and university supervisors. Technology can increase the number of supervisors for an intern by using remote supervision with webcams.

The questions are: How can we provide more classroom experience for our preservice teachers? How can we provide quality experiences for our preservice teachers? Today's college students are struggling financially, and it is not reasonable to extend their college experience and expenses for another year for clinical practice. Today's college students are also technologically savvy. They are willing to use technology in their classes and learn through digital means. Incorporating remote supervision and other digital approaches to clinical practice can improve the quality and quantity of the experience.

These are not the only solutions. Above all, the teacher preparation facul-ties need to brainstorm ways to meet the needs of their candidates using new and different approaches. Today's teacher preparation programs should not look like they did yesterday.

School District Participation in Preparation

Universities and school districts both have enormous jobs to do, for time, money, and resources are all precious. However, both universities and school districts are working toward the same goal of an educated and productive citizenry. Teacher preparation programs are working toward producing effec-tive, productive teacher leaders for our schools. School districts need those effective teacher leaders in order to meet their goals for productive and educated citizens. In the past, though, there has been little conversation be-tween the two entities about their common goals. It is now important for us to work together.

Colleges of education and teacher preparation programs need to invite school districts and schools to the conversations about new teachers. Prepara-tion programs need to know what the school districts need in terms of new teachers. Who better to give input into what a new teacher needs to know than a future employer? School districts see the trends in demographics and issues in classrooms earlier than the university. These insights can be valu-able when teacher preparation programs are considering changes to curricu-lum and clinical practices. By working together, the two partners can create a more effective and better prepared new teacher.

CONCLUSIONS

The experiences of the new teacher are challenging to educational reform. How can a new teacher make a change in the system while trying to survive the first few years? By preparing a more effective teacher through quality clinical practices with the help of school districts, the new teacher is better equipped to meet the challenges of the first year of teaching. Mentoring that individual teacher not only through the first year but through the first few years can continue the growth of the teacher to become a teacher leader and change agent for education.

REFERENCES

Goodlad, J. I. (1984). *A place called school: Prospects for the future.* New York: McGraw-Hill.
Ingersoll, R. (2001). Teacher turnover and teacher shortages: An organizational analysis. *American Educational Research Journal, 38*(3), 499–534.

National Council for Accreditation of Teacher Education. (2010). *Transforming teacher education through clinical practice: A national strategy to prepare effective teachers.* Washington, DC: Author.
Schlichte, J., Yssel, N., & Merbler, J. (2005). Pathways to burnout: Case studies in teacher isolation and alienation. *Preventing School Failure, 50*(1), 35–40.

Chapter Three

Leaving the Profession

Research supports that a great number of teachers leave the profession within the first five years (Ingersoll, 2001). This population is interesting in relation to educational reform. The reasons for attrition are varied, but the bottom line is that a significant number of young teachers leave the profession each year. I was one of these teachers.

The narratives in this chapter offer two differing rationales for leaving the profession. One is leaving education entirely, while the other is moving on in education. It is important to think about the motivations behind leaving the school system. On one hand, the profession may be strengthened by the attrition of teachers who are ineffective; on the other hand, teachers who want to make a difference in education in another venue need to be nurtured.

The obstacles to change from this perspective are loss of momentum in the change process, ineffective use of funding, and isolation. The strengths include entrance of dedicated teachers to other educational arenas, loss of ineffective teachers, and evaluation of the educational system. The final section in the chapter addresses how we need to move forward with mentoring, protection, and empowerment.

NARRATIVE

I Lost This Fight

Miss Bradford could not contain her excitement. She was going to get paid to teach students something she loved. Every day she would get to share her love for drama and plays and words and characters with enthusiastic, eager young talent. Smith Valley High School had just hired her as the new theater teacher. She would have five drama classes, one technical theater class, and a conference period. She was in heaven. She had already updated her social network profile and sent text messages of the news to family and friends. Two months from now she would begin to mold young artists.

Miss Bradford maintained her enthusiasm into the first six weeks of school. But then reality began to creep in. As part of her responsibilities, she was to produce one play per semester. In the fall, she began reading plays and had some great ideas for a production that would allow for many students to participate not only as actors but also as technical help with lights and sound.

When she took the teaching position, she knew the high school did not have a performance space but was told the cafetorium at the junior high would be available to use for performances. She contacted the junior high principal for keys to the school and access to the light and sound boards. The principal gave her keys but said there was no sound board and as far as lights went, there were switches on the wall, but she should only use regular lights and not the stage lights. "Well, okay," she thought, "I can work around all that." Miss Bradford continued to work on the production with only a slight decrease in enthusiasm.

Teaching drama is messy and chaotic. It is noisy and busy. Rehearsals are even more chaotic. Miss Bradford's production had been adapted to meet the challenges of no sound system and limited lighting, but she had a cast of seventeen students. Scenes ranged from two actors onstage to all seventeen. At any given time there were students waiting for their turn in the audience. These students worked on homework, ran lines, practiced blocking, and talked. Even though rehearsals were after school, the chaos of the production did not sit well with the principal. A week before the production was to open, he pulled Miss Bradford aside.

"Miss Bradford, I appreciate that you are a new teacher and may not have complete control of your students, but if you do not get control soon, I will have to revoke your access to the cafetorium," he said.

Miss Bradford was stunned. After closing her mouth and blinking a few times, she replied. "Oh, well. We are almost done with our production. You see, the final week is crazy with the final rehearsals, but it will settle down soon."

"I have been watching you these past five weeks, and I don't think it will. In fact, I think this situation is too distracting to my teachers and after-school students. You will need to find somewhere else to have your spring production," he said as he turned on his heel and left.

At that, Miss Bradford decided to think about a new space later. She steeled herself and finished her fall production with a little less enthusiasm.

Spring came quickly, and Miss Bradford approached her principal about the best place to have the spring production. Right away he suggested the old auditorium at the elementary school. The school board was trying to get it marked as a historical building. Miss Bradford was relieved until she saw the space. The stage was wonderful. However, there were no lights or sound systems. The curtains had been attacked by moths, but luckily there were windows, so natural light came in.

Miss Bradford cast her play and began rehearsals. Only then she realized that there were no bathrooms and no heat or air conditioning in the building.

Miss Bradford approached the principal about what to do. He assured her the space was great and she could have all her productions there next year. She asked about renovations, and he assured her they really wanted to clean up the auditorium, but the money they had was going toward a new football field next year.

Miss Bradford steeled herself once again and finished the production with some enthusiasm, but she finished the school year with none.

NARRATIVE

This Is It?

Mr. Rivers liked eating his lunch in the teacher's lounge. He had been warned by his college professors to stay out of the teacher's lounge to avoid griping and gossiping, but his high school campus was really a great place to work and learn. Many times in the teacher's lounge Mr. Rivers would ask other English teachers different approaches to topics if he was finding his students were not getting it. All of the other English teachers were supportive and open.

It was a Tuesday in late April. As all teachers know, spring fever is a real condition to adolescents and teenagers. Standardized testing was over, but there were still a few weeks left in the semester. The seniors had regressed to acting like kindergarteners. Lessons were hit and miss. Everyone was counting down the days until summer vacation, but all teachers knew it was part of the cycle of the school year.

This Tuesday, Mr. Rivers took his lunch of ham and Swiss on wheat, one pickle, and two chocolate chip cookies to the teacher's lounge. He was ready for a few minutes away from the students and looking forward to talking about the upcoming community fund-raiser. Mrs. Jackson was already sitting on the tired old sofa while two novice teachers were chatting quietly at the round, wobbly table by the vending machine. Mr. Rivers took a seat on the other end of the sofa and asked Mrs. Jackson where everyone was.

"Well, John's wife had an asthma attack and he left to take her to the ER, and Sharon is having a study session in her room. I am not sure where Tom and Lisa are," she replied.

"Wow. I hope his wife is all right." Mr. Rivers knew that she had a tendency to visit the ER at least once a month and was not overly concerned. "What is going on with you?" he asked Mrs. Jackson.

"Not too much," she said. She seemed a little quiet. Usually Mrs. Jackson was the cheerleader for the faculty. She had been teaching English to seniors for eighteen years and loved every minute of it. Today she lacked her regular enthusiasm. She sat sunk down in the sofa, picking the crust of her chicken salad sandwich.

Mr. Rivers was somewhat unsettled to see his role model so down. He was at a loss for words but decided to try anyway.

"You seem out of sorts. Is there anything I can help you with today?" he asked.

"Out of sorts. I like that. I think I have been out of sorts for some time." She looked around and seemed to be through talking until she turned directly to Mr. Rivers. "Did you always want to be a teacher?" she asked. Her stare and concentration indicated there was a great deal riding on his answer.

"Well, I did want to be a clown when I was younger." He paused for her laughter, but there was none. Clearing his throat, he said, "Yeah. I always did. Didn't you?"

The tears were unexpected. Mrs. Jackson sat perfectly still as large tears rolled down her cheeks into her lap. Mr. Rivers expected to see a small pool of water in her lap soon.

"No, I didn't. I wanted to be a writer. I started teaching to make ends meet while I wrote. Then suddenly I was married and a mother, and we had a new house. And now I can't get out. I can't leave. I have to teach to take care of my family, and I love my family. You know? I love them. I would not trade them for anything. But sometimes I still grieve over the death of my dream," she said.

And then she wrapped up her sandwich in napkins and threw it in the trash can by the door as she left. The door slowly closed, and Mr. Rivers could barely hear the latch click. He was thinking about his answer earlier. He had lied. He had said what he thought she wanted to hear. More importantly, he said what *he* thought he wanted to hear.

Mr. Rivers did not feel like eating his cookies. He handed them to the new teachers on his way out of the teacher's lounge. Back in his classroom, he opened the bottom right-hand drawer in his desk and pulled out a tattered manila folder with a sticky note and jottings on the cover. He opened the folder and read the first of thirty-six pages. His first complete short story. As he closed the folder, he removed the sticky note with an e-mail address written on it.

He woke up his computer, opened the e-mail program, and began to write.

OBSTACLES TO EDUCATIONAL REFORM

Retention of teachers is challenging for districts and administrations. Although there is research on retention and strategies to maintain the teacher population, little addresses the implications of continued turnover in the profession. In relation to educational reform, the high rate of teachers leaving the profession can hinder or even undermine any innovations for change. Three implications that need to be considered are the loss of the change momentum, how funds are lost when turnover is high, and feelings of isolation in the faculty who stay.

Loss of Change Momentum

In order for the change process to work, the individuals involved need to have time to make sense of the innovations or implementations (Sarason, 1996). In practical terms, the classroom teacher needs to understand the changes in curriculum or instruction, think about the ways in which her classroom will be different, experiment with the strategy, and come to terms with the differences as she accepts the change. This process is personal and takes time. As campuses deal with attrition of faculty, this personal sense making is delayed and at times is even deleted. As the open faculty positions are filled with new personnel, the teachers are expected to adjust to the change immediately. There is no time left for buy-in.

Additionally, the administration struggles to find the resources to support the new faculty members. For example, a middle school campus chose to implement a new character education program. There were thirty-seven teachers on campus. During the beginning phase of the change, all the teachers had access to three different programs the school was considering. A small group of teachers tried out the curriculum and had focus group discussions. Faculty and administration decided together which program to adopt after eighteen months of discussion.

The new program would be phased in by adding two grade levels each year. In the summer prior to the grade-level implementation, those teachers would participate in training. The whole school would be using the curriculum in three years. However, in that time, fourteen of the teachers have left and been replaced. The new teachers that have been hired to teach in the grades that have already implemented the program have no training because funds were allocated for grade-level use. The implementation may be finished in four and a half years, but there are holes in classrooms where teachers have left.

Funding Redirection

The hiring process for schools is an expensive one. Not only does the process take monetary assets to complete, it also takes time. Many districts will involve the principal, assistant principal, and faculty members in the hiring process as well as the human resources department. The issue is not that districts have to hire teachers; that will always be the case. The issue is that districts have to hire greater numbers of teachers to account for the teachers who leave the profession, especially in the first five years. The attrition of teachers in the first five years of service leads to a dearth of teachers that make it to veteran status. In essence, the teachers needed to mentor and support our novice teachers are not there because they have left the profession early.

With this cycle of attrition and hiring, the professional development funds will continue to be allocated to bringing the new teachers up to speed while very little will be spent acclimating them to innovations or the change process. In these economic times, schools are struggling to find the funding to operate, and professional development is not the priority for many districts. School faculties will continue to need support, the money will be directed toward that, and what little is left over will be for the subset of new teachers. Financially, schools are operating on a reduced budget throughout much of the nation; attrition only adds to the financial stresses of schools.

Isolation

Isolation has consistently been a challenge to retention of teachers. Indeed, the issue of isolation alone leads to many teachers feeling dissatisfied in their careers, and it can even lead to burnout. This isolation can lead to teachers leaving the profession or transitioning out of the classroom. Two major aspects of isolation affect educational reform: isolation from others and isolation from ideas.

As Ingersoll (2001) suggests, the teaching profession leaves the adult professional isolated from any other adult professionals. On any given day, a teacher may have a short five-minute conversation with an adult and eight hours of interaction with children, adolescents, and teenagers. Weeks may go by with no significant interaction among professionals. Generally, the structure of schooling in the United States does not build in time for professional collaboration. Several strategies have been implemented in recent decades to overcome some of the isolation, such as teaming and coteaching. However, in many schools it is still one teacher and twenty-five students in the classroom for the majority of the day.

The other aspect of isolation is isolation from ideas, and this is particularly important when talking about educational reform. When teachers are enmeshed in the day-to-day work of teaching, there is little time for philosophical discussions or brainstorming of new innovations. Conversations among teachers often focus on helping each other with strategies for student learning, ideas about classroom management, and, at times, emotional support to make it through the day, week, and school year.

Classroom teachers are removed from the types of idealistic conversations they had when they were still preservice teachers in college. Conversations about educational reform and school change will not happen organically in schools; a catalyst is needed to begin these conversations. While teachers are isolated from other professionals and environments that support ideas of reform, the risk of burnout and attrition becomes high.

STRENGTHS OF THIS PERSPECTIVE

Interestingly, there is a positive side to teachers leaving the classroom. First, some of those professionals who leave the classroom move on to other areas of education, including educational leadership and teacher education. Also, a percentage of the teachers who leave will be the teachers who are not effective in the classroom, allowing more effective teachers to replace them. The teachers who leave can also offer a critical evaluation of the educational system as they share their reasons for leaving.

Mobility to Other Areas of Education

One possible career move for teachers leaving the classroom is to move into a different area of education. Many states require the principal and school counselor to have a set number of years of experience in the classroom before transitioning to an administrative role. At any time then, there is a group of teachers who are planning on moving into more leadership roles in their careers. These teachers complete their requisite three to five years in the classroom while continuing coursework in graduate studies.

There are also the veteran teachers who want a change and move into administration or counseling. These professionals are a great benefit to the educational reform movement. They are given power to make changes by the definition of their new positions, and they are able to draw on their experiences as classroom teachers to make meaningful and effective changes to schools.

The second important group to leave the profession is the individuals who choose to move into higher education. A natural progression in career is to go from being a classroom teacher to preparing classroom teachers. Many teacher educators have been classroom teachers prior to their tenure in a higher education institution. Again, these career changers bring a unique perspective to educational reform. They know what is it is like to be the classroom teacher year after year and the challenges the classroom teachers face daily. By drawing on their previous career experience, these teacher educators can prepare preservice teachers to be reform minded, continuous learners and future leaders of the profession. The loss of these teachers from the public schools is the gain of teacher education programs at the university.

Loss of Ineffective Teachers

Another benefit of teacher attrition is that some of the teachers who leave are ineffective teachers. Obviously, it is impossible to quantify the number of teachers who both leave during the early years and are ineffective, but a portion of the population is the teachers who have become unhappy, burned out, or fed up. By no means is waiting for ineffective teachers to leave of their own accord the best way to deal with classroom issues, but it is a positive spin on attrition.

The first years are a critical developmental stage for teacher identity (Beauchamp & Thomas, 2009). It is also a time where there is high turnover in teaching positions. Teacher preparation programs offer a variety of clinical practices and field experiences for preservice teachers to get a better understanding as to what a day in school entails, but this is not always adequate preparation. Teacher preparation programs and schools need to work together to support new teachers through induction and mentoring programs. These programs can help support an increase in the effectiveness of new teachers or address some of the weaker areas in teaching as well as provide opportunities to reflect on teachers' expectations. Through these joint efforts and support, the teachers may grow into effective classroom leaders or realize that their talents are better applied in another setting.

Evaluation of the System

Many companies require employees to complete an exit interview or survey. These may cover a myriad of issues and facets of the company, but it is data that proves useful to the company in future decisions. In American education, we are overlooking the exit interview as a data-gathering opportunity.

People who leave the profession have ideas about what could have changed to make them stay or simply make their experiences better. It is a perspective of evaluation that is easily overlooked. When reading about educational reform, the writers are professors, researchers, legislators, and administrators; rarely do we get the teacher perspective, and even more elusive is the perspective of the one who left the profession. The teachers who move on to administrator or higher education positions no doubt take that experience and use it to inform future decisions in their new work. However, the teachers who leave education entirely are lost. If education professionals could hear those perspectives, ideas, comments, and criticisms, it may prove very valuable in the reformation process.

MOVING FORWARD

A great deal has been written about overcoming attrition in the profession, but there are some strategies that may be more effective when discussing attrition and educational reform together. New and fairly new teachers need to be mentored in an effective, consistent, and extended way. In addition, the new teachers need to be protected from overloaded classes and the most challenging classes on campus. Finally, all teachers need to be empowered as teacher leaders through professional development and continuing education opportunities.

Extended Mentoring Programs

Mentoring programs have shown to be beneficial to new teachers (Strong, 2005); however, effective programs take dedicated time and resources. In most districts, the burden of sustaining mentorship programs is borne by the district. The majority of universities end their preparation at graduation. Some universities and districts have a professional development school relationship, but that does not necessarily meet the needs of the new teachers. What is really needed for the education industry is an induction and mentoring program supported by the states, districts, and university preparation programs together.

Programs of this type would look very different from the current mentoring programs in place today. Universities and districts could collaborate to create an induction program that would support the new teacher in an effective and practical way. Although teacher preparation programs are doing the best they can, there are still gaps in experience that need to be addressed as a new teacher, not a preservice teacher. In addition, school districts have unique expectations for their teachers. Principals and professors could sit down and identify topics and areas of preparation for both the university and the district. Time and resources could be pooled to provide the needed professional development and guidance for the new teachers in a safe and collaborative environment.

Protection of New Teachers

Unfortunately, many new teachers are assigned to the most difficult classes to teach. Many new teachers are given classes with highly diverse populations and learning styles. These types of classrooms are not filled with students who cannot learn, but with students who need a teacher with many classroom management strategies and varied instructional practices. In reality, new teachers are coming out of preparation programs prepared in one or two educational approaches. All preparation programs have some instructional bias, whether it is constructivism or coteaching. The argument here is not to force preparation programs to address more education approaches, but to give the new teachers time to acquire them on the job through professional development and collaboration with veteran teachers.

In addition, new teachers need to be protected from overcrowded classrooms and "dumping grounds," or classes the students get assigned to just to get through the year. These types of classes are challenging for many veteran teachers. If we can protect new teachers and provide effective professional development, then they will be better qualified to meet the needs of the students in these courses and will succeed, just as their students will. To send new teachers into challenging classrooms without the skills needed is a setup for student failure and teacher attrition.

Empowerment of Teacher Leaders

Finally, all teachers need to be empowered as teacher leaders. True systemic reform will not be successful or sustainable until classroom teachers work together to make changes to the system. Teachers can make a difference not only in their classrooms but also in their schools, districts, states, and profession. To empower teachers is a systemic change in itself. School districts cannot do it alone, and neither can universities. The message that teachers are important and critical to changing the education system must be heard first in the university preparation programs and then in the schools if not simultaneously.

Teacher preparation programs will have to embrace the idea of educational reform. Oftentimes, educational change is addressed as something that happens to teachers, something to prepare for or brace against, but definitely not something to initiate. Professors will have to give examples and ways for teachers to act as leaders and change agents. Principals will have to look to their own faculty for ideas and innovations. The classroom teacher becomes the expert and the resource; she becomes the leader of change and not an obstacle to overcome in the change process. Schools and university programs would look very different.

CONCLUSIONS

Teachers who leave the profession offer opportunities for reflection on our profession and also a chance to grow. As a profession, we want new teachers to stay to become veteran teachers, and to make this happen, the issues of this group must be addressed. Yes, some new teachers need to leave to move up toward administration in education, and yes, some do need to leave the profession, but the ones that have potential need to be nurtured into staying and growing into the teacher leaders of tomorrow through professional development, protection, and empowerment.

REFERENCES

Beauchamp, C., & Thomas, L. (2009). Understanding teacher identity: An overview of issues in the literature and implication for teacher education. *Cambridge Journal of Education, 39*(2), 175–189.

Ingersoll, R. (2001). Teacher turnover and teacher shortages: An organizational analysis. *American Educational Research Journal, 38*(3), 499–534.

Sarason, S. (1996). *Revisiting the culture of school and the problem of change.* New York: Teachers College Press.

Strong, M. (2005). Mentoring new teachers to increase retention. Research Brief 05-01. Retrieved from http://community.newteachercenter.org/sites/default/files/ntc/main/resources/BRF_MentoringNewTeacherstoIncreaseRetention.pdf

Chapter Four

Life as a Graduate Student

Approximately 1 percent of the population has a doctorate degree (US Census Bureau, 2011). The people included in this 1 percent have had a diversity of experiences in different university settings, from urban to rural, and have been exposed to research intensively focused on teaching. The experience of the doctoral process shapes and molds the academic for the future. For teacher education, it is important not to overlook this formative time for the future teacher educator.

The narratives in this chapter detail experiences of a doctoral student engaged with two very different faculty members who both shape the perspective of the student in relation to change and educational reformation. In order for change to occur in any institution or system, the agents must be prepared to implement and guide the system through the process. In higher education, that means including change theory in the curriculum for future academics. The discussion in this chapter focuses on theory and practicality of that preparation.

The obstacles to change from this perspective include a distance from the reality of the classroom, an imbalance of theoretical and practical preparation, and the lack of power. Strengths include the abundance of ideals, the constant engagement in critical discussion, and collaborative environments.

NARRATIVE

A Student Again

Meg felt butterflies in her stomach. She was sitting in a classroom with eight other people about to begin her doctoral studies. She did not sleep the night before, and she expected to have a headache by the afternoon like she always had when she was too excited. She just couldn't believe that she was a student again. She was back in school—one of her favorite places in the world.

Meg had been a public school teacher for five years. She taught high school English in a rural area. Recently she married her college boyfriend and moved for his job. Her only requirement was that she be able to get her doctorate. So here she was, newly married and newly enrolled. She played with the small solitaire diamond on her left hand as she watched the other eight students.

There were five men and three other women. Most of them appeared to be much older than Meg. She was just about to ask the older lady next to her about her background when the door opened and a dark-haired, slightly stooped man in his late fifties entered hastily. He stopped at the top of the U-shaped desks, threw down a pile of papers, and pushed up his glasses.

"This is curriculum theory and anyone expecting a different class should leave." He paused. "All right, let's get to work."

He quickly passed out a syllabus that was as thick as a magazine. "This is our contract. I will require each of you to adhere to the contract. All assignments are outlined in here with due dates and expectations. Your first reading is Tyler's book, and it is due next week. This afternoon we will have a preassessment to see how much you know about curriculum." And with that, he passed around another packet of papers as thick as a catalog.

"You have an hour," he said as he left the room. Immediately, pens were put to paper. There were no sounds except breathing and writing. For Meg, the questions were challenging but not ridiculous. At the end of the hour she was proud of her responses, and at the end of the hour the professor reappeared.

"Let's have your work. I will evaluate it and create a remediation plan for those who need leveling work. Now I want each of you to tell me why you are here," said the professor.

Each student took a turn relating a desire to help more children or grow into a new position or finish a doctorate to keep their current job. Meg waited anxiously for her turn. The butterflies were back, and she kept her hand on her rings.

"I was a classroom teacher for five years and I loved it. I think I am here because I want to get a doctorate to prove something to myself. If, in the process, I learn more about my field and I can enhance my impact on students, then all the better. I just want to know more," Meg said. She felt certain everyone was quietly laughing.

"Interesting," said the professor. "I can't wait to read your analyses."

At that moment, Meg was hooked. She waited all week for class with the professor. She actually read the assigned readings and wrote thoughtfully and thoroughly. She was engaged in an academic dialogue that she could not imagine living without. Each week, each topic uncovered some unknown truth or question. The depth of the knowledge the professor had was unsettling. The questions he asked never failed to push her thinking to a new level.

Simply put, she was engaged and learning all the time. And she loved every minute.

NARRATIVE

Challenge to Become Myself

Kim was in her second semester of her doctoral program when she took a class from Dr. Blanton. The class was a theory class about instructional design. She was not very excited about the class, but other students had said good things about the professor.

At the first class meeting, Dr. Blanton came in and sat down. He had a yellow legal pad and a pen. "I don't like to hand out the syllabus on the first meeting; I like to get to know you," Dr. Blanton said.

As in most other classes, the students introduced themselves one by one. This time, however, Dr. Blanton asked questions. "What do you want to do with that degree?" "Where will you see yourself in five years?" "How will you use what you are learning?" The introductory conversations were interesting, and soon the class was over.

At the next class meeting there was a syllabus. Assignments included a journal and a final project. There were no directions for either assignment. Kim asked about how they were to approach the assignments.

"I want you to keep a journal of what you are thinking about. What are you questioning? What makes sense to you? What is still unclear? Whatever you think is important to write about, put it in your journal. For the final project, I want you to create a model representing instructional design," Dr. Blanton said and did not elaborate any further.

As the class went on, Dr. Blanton kept bringing in his legal pad and pen. He would take up journals and read and return them with no grades, only more questions. His questions in class became more and more tailored for each student. Kim's friend Mel was a science education student, and Dr. Blanton queried him specific pedagogical questions related to that field.

During one class meeting, students were discussing the disconnection between the theory of modeling as an instructional method and its lack of use in university courses. Kim spoke up and said that it didn't make sense to teach students to use something but not show them how to use it by modeling it for them. Dr. Blanton asked her some probing questions that challenged her. Finally, he asked, "How would you teach it?"

Kim was taken aback for a moment but quickly came back with a plan for using real case studies as the basis for classroom management. Dr. Blanton asked if she was a teaching assistant, and she said yes. Then the discussion moved on.

During the week, Kim got an e-mail message from Dr. Blanton asking her to come see him during office hours. She thought it odd but knocked on his office door at precisely 2:00 on Wednesday afternoon. He called for her to come in. As she entered, she was surprised by the amount of paper and the number of books piled precariously throughout the office; she could just make out the top of his head behind his desk. He stood and came around the desk, clearing two chairs. "Sit down, please."

"Ms. Smith, I wanted to talk to you about an opportunity. I have spoken with the department chair, and she has approved you to teach classroom management next semester instead of the regular introduction course the assistants teach. I was very intrigued by your answers in class last week, and I wanted to give you an opportunity to try out your approach. What do you think?" Dr. Blanton said.

Kim was stunned and speechless. Finally, she heard herself saying that she was definitely interested and would love to work with him and teach the course.

"Good. We'll get the details straightened out later. Thanks for coming by," Dr. Blanton said before returning to the mountains of paper.

Kim could not believe her luck. But as she thought about it, she realized, Dr. Blanton was only building on what had been discussed in the classroom. He was making connections between the theory and the application. This was the first time he created an opportunity for her, but it would not be the last.

In the end, it was always Dr. Blanton who advocated for the students.

OBSTACLES TO EDUCATIONAL REFORM

This perspective is unique in that the doctoral candidate is in preparation to become a teacher educator and the experiences are more fluid and diverse than some of the other perspectives. Yet for that very reason this perspective has significant obstacles as well as strengths. The obstacles relate to the cocooned atmosphere of the academy, the intense focus on the theoretical, and the impotence that accompanies the idealism of these candidates.

Disconnection from the Reality of Education

Although many doctoral candidates for teacher education programs have spent time teaching in PK–12 settings, the acculturation to the academy does not highlight these experiences; rather, the experiences are looked at as a requirement for entrance but not an asset for success. In essence, the doctoral candidates begin again in the pursuit of the doctoral degree; previous experiences are required but not integrated into the curriculum.

This leads to a disconnection between the public schools and the doctoral candidates in teacher education.

The coursework and research that is undertaken in a doctoral program is important and integral for the preparation of high-quality, effective teacher educators. Professors of education should be able to conduct and direct research, be knowledgeable and current in their field, and effectively teach the undergraduate and graduate students. It takes the extended experience of a doctoral program to do that. However, professors of education should also be able to connect to schools and create partnerships with districts and campuses.

Many doctoral programs use their doctoral candidates in conjunction with field-based courses or partnerships. Most of the time this experience is limited; the candidate may supervise students or teach on-site. What the candidate needs are experiences that will build a skill set that allows her to work with classroom teachers and district personnel as an education professor at her future university.

Theoretical Preparation versus Practical

Preparation of teacher educators often mirrors the preparation of our classroom teachers. There is a great deal of theory about the field shared, discussed, or covered, but sometimes the educator is expected to learn a great deal on the job. During doctoral studies, some candidates have the opportunity to work as teaching or research assistants, but a required interaction with their future classroom population is not included. The preservice teachers are all required to complete a field experience or clinical practice of some sort, but our teacher educators are not.

Foundational information about education and theory about learning, curriculum, and instruction are important for the success of our teacher educators. One of the signatures of doctoral programs is the depth of knowledge that is afforded the candidate. This continued focus on content and theory allows for the development of critical thinking and evaluation skills that are necessary for ethical and effective research and scholarship. The argument is not against that type of preparation, but that our traditional preparation of teacher educators allows for a disconnection from the reality of schools by the lack of practical preparation, including field experiences.

Impotence

The lack of power is not unique to this perspective, but it is probably most detrimental. The preparation of teacher educators provides a fertile environment for brainstorming ideas for reform and innovation of teaching and education. Traditionally, these ideas could be explored through the dissertation process of most programs. Even so, the doctoral candidate has little power to make any significant change in education or schools. Even the most innovative and promising dissertation study still has to be read and disseminated for other programs or professors to begin to think of implementing such an idea. The new assistant professor can draw on his research and disseminate it in many ways, yet the changes at the classroom level are still years away.

Understandably, the doctoral candidate has limited power due to the fact that she is still in a learning phase. Doctoral studies take time, and the growth and change in professional and sometimes personal thinking is slow but drastic. This period of professional development is ripe with creativity and collaboration opportunities. Free thinking, brainstorming, and challenging debates abound in the classrooms. Unfortunately, this may be the last time the teacher educator will have the freedom, time, and support to investigate ideas and challenge colleagues without the pressures of gaining tenure and promotion. The obstacle is the lack of power to implement the ideas and innovations that abound in these doctoral programs.

STRENGTHS OF THIS PERSPECTIVE

As with the other perspectives, the perspective of the doctoral candidate offers some interesting strengths. In order to really effect any changes to education in the United States, each perspective's strengths will need to be used. Doctoral candidates offer an unending supply of innovations and ideas due to the untainted mindset full of ideals, the critical perspective of fresh minds, and the constant creativity of a collaborative environment.

Ideals

For many doctoral candidates, the years of study in a program are a time of optimism and idealism. Many students in preservice programs feel the same way; there is an excitement of possibilities and endless opportunities. Then experience in the profession turns many of those idealistic teachers into jaded cynics. In this phase of professional life, the doctoral candidate is quite like the preservice teacher. Optimism abounds. Even if the doctoral candidate comes from a jaded classroom experience, the doctoral years open new possibilities for change and making a difference. Optimism is restored. The challenge is then to capitalize on and support that idealism.

The major strength of this perspective is the untapped idealism. Candidates should be nurtured into considering new possibilities and approaches to traditional methods and theories. The asset of the academy is that it is a safe environment for brainstorming and asking "what if." Professors like the ones depicted in the narratives are critical to the preparation of future teacher educators and to the improvement of the education system in the United States in general. Professors in teacher education and doctoral programs must be engaged and excited and willing to challenge their students and candidates. Later chapters will discuss in detail the strengths and obstacles of the professoriate.

Critical Thinking

An additional strength of this perspective is critical thinking. Fullan (1991) uses the metaphor of an outsider looking down on our educational system. The boundaries and constructs we take for granted are then put under the microscope for examination. Why do schools close in the summer? Why do we start at 8:00 and end at 3:00? Why are students separated by age? Candidates in doctoral programs have the opportunity to act as such an outsider and critically evaluate the system.

Most doctoral candidates in education fields have some experience in the American public school system. Their experiences range from a few years of teaching to a career's worth of experience. However, when they transition back to the role of a student, they can take the experiences and examine them through the theories and frameworks of the doctoral curriculum. It is as if a new filter has been added to their schema that lets them look at their previous work in a completely new way. Candidates are also supported by professors who continually challenge them to think and evaluate on their own. This combination gives the system an enormous resource.

These candidates are a source of critical insight and analysis of schooling. This perspective is powerful in that the candidates know about education through firsthand experience in the classrooms, and they are synthesizing that experience with the deep content knowledge from a doctoral program to come up with innovations, approaches, and critiques of the system of education. No other perspective is as pure in its assessment of the system as this one is.

Collaborative Environment

Education professionals in general consider themselves more collaborative than their counterparts in many other professions. This is especially true throughout the doctoral process. First, many programs will admit candidates as cohorts, which begins a collaborative environment almost immediately. Other programs may not, but the rigor of the programs unites candidates through peer editing groups, study groups, research groups, and teaching assistant groups. Unlike undergraduate courses full of lecture, doctoral courses include more discussion and exchange of ideas, all of which lead to a more collaborative environment for the candidate.

Teachers and educators are collaborative professionals. In public schools, teachers share lesson plans, resources, and ideas. Professors share syllabi, books, and articles and collaborate on research and scholarship. Unfortunately, pressures in both the public school and academia do not allow for in-depth collaboration at times.

Time is limited to, at best, a shared conference period in most public schools, and for professors the time demands of class and writing limit their time for conversing and sharing ideas. Although collaborative environments are important, the time and resources needed to foster and maintain such a productive environment are limited. The doctoral process is the last place in the professional timeline that the collaborative environment is unfettered and unlimited.

MOVING FORWARD

Based on the specific obstacles and strengths of this perspective, there are several ways in which the contribution to educational reform can be enhanced. Universities need to help make meaningful connections between the school districts and the educational preparation programs. The professional associations of teacher education and content areas need to be utilized for mentoring the novice professional. Finally, the doctoral programs need to prepare their candidates for the demands of the academy.

Make Connections in Schools and EPPs

Connections between public schools and universities must be the major focus for effective change to schooling today. Our preservice teachers need the connections to field sites for practical application of theory and strategy. Our classroom teachers need the connections for support, professional development, and collaboration. The doctoral candidates need the connections for learning how to manage and grow relationships for clinical practice and professional development as well as for having a place for field experiences. The relationship must be an all-encompassing, integrated effort for both the schools and universities.

Professional development schools (PDS) are one approach to the growth of such a relationship. The National Association for Professional Development Schools (NAPDS) has nine essential components for a PDS partnership, which include a shared mission, professional development, resources, commitment to innovation, and more (2008). This type of relationship is beneficial for teacher preparation; however, most PDS programs are not all encompassing.

Most PDS relationships focus on the preservice teacher. A part of the relationship of a PDS should also include educational leaders and the teacher educators of tomorrow. Some doctoral candidates are afforded the opportunity to work with schools through their graduate assistantship, but many others miss out on that work. A required field component or internship focused on building relationships, sharing resources, and uniting missions would be greatly beneficial for the teacher educator.

Mentoring from Professional Associations

As an academic, one is expected to participate in professional associations at a state, national, and even international level. Two of the major professional organizations for teacher education are the American Association of Colleges for Teacher Education (AACTE) and the Association for Teacher Educators (ATE). AACTE offers institutional membership for colleges of education while ATE is an individual membership organization. Both organizations do great things for teacher education in distinctly different ways.

However, both could encourage more doctoral students to participate in the organization and take advantage of conferences and professional development offered by both. The American Educational Research Association (AERA) is another professional organization that allows for participation by doctoral students focusing primarily on research. In addition, there are many content area–specific associations to which doctoral candidates have access.

These organizations have a vested interest in the future of teacher education. (If they began by fostering a relationship with the doctoral candidate in some capacity, it may make the efforts of reform and change easier to manage since the doctoral candidate would be prepared for the challenges of becoming a teacher educator.) In a following chapter, the perspective of the assistant professor will be discussed and the concept of mentoring will be revisited. For this perspective, having early entry into a professional organization with an interest in their perspective would benefit future teacher educators greatly.

Preparation for the Academy

Preparation for the academy differs from mentoring by professional associations. Professional associations are supporting professional development in relation to scholarship, reform, and research. The preparation for the academy needs to come from the doctoral faculty in the education programs. As stated previously, each individual doctoral candidate has a different experience, from attending only night classes for years to teaching in the program on a daily basis. The variety of experience results in a varied level of preparedness for the academy.

Each university has its own set of tenure and promotion guidelines and its own mission statement. Yet there is an expectation of research, service, and teaching at almost every institution. Most doctoral candidates understand the concept of teaching and are prepared for classroom instruction. Some doctoral candidates are well prepared to research and have an agenda prepared before their first tenure-track position. Few candidates understand the demands of service and what service means to different institutions.

It is almost impossible to convey the demands of the first three years of an assistant professor tenure-track position to a doctoral candidate swimming in his own dissertation research. But we must try. If future teacher educators understand more clearly the demands of the academy and are equipped with skills to help balance the demands of teaching, service, and scholarship, then change and educational reformation may be easier to accomplish. Everyone will need to make changes and sustain initiatives, including the new assistant professor. If some of the on-the-job training is done in the doctoral studies, more can be accomplished in the first three years as a faculty member.

CONCLUSIONS

The perspective of the doctoral student is unique and vital to the educational reform movement. The candidate will be the future teacher educator, and as such, the preparation of the candidate needs to be well planned and beneficial to his success in the future. By drawing on the strengths of idealism, critical thinking, and collaboration, changes can be made in teacher preparation. By calling on professional associations and doctoral faculty to help prepare and support the doctoral candidate during his transition, more time is given to meaningful work instead of acclimation to the profession. All in all, this particular perspective is very promising for the future of education.

REFERENCES

Fullan, M. (1991). *The new meaning of educational change*. New York: Teachers College Press.
National Association for Professional Development Schools. (2008). *What it means to be a professional development school*. Columbia, SC: Author.
US Census Bureau. (2011). *Current population survey, 2011 annual social and economic supplement*. Washington, DC: Author.

Chapter Five

Life after Graduate School

As the economic times have turned in the United States, the positions in higher education have been affected. Many doctoral and master's graduates are challenged to find faculty positions in the academy. In an effort to gain entry into higher education, many newly minted doctors turn to adjunct positions. This perspective is important as budgets get cut in many universities and departments turn to cheaper alternatives than the tenure-track professor to teach and include more and more adjuncts in instructional roles.

The narratives in the chapter reflect the isolation and disconnection of the adjunct professor and the varied pathways to a tenure-track position. Adjunct positions can be an entry to the professoriate, but they can also be an area of stunted growth and loneliness. The narratives explore these issues related to adjunct positions.

The obstacles to educational reform are many for this perspective. Programmatic issues include the high number of adjuncts teaching undergraduate courses and the disconnection between adjunct and tenure-track faculty. For the individual, the lack of opportunities and the financial compensation can be challenging. These challenges act as barriers to reform momentum in higher education.

On the other hand, adjunct faculty members have a strength in the insight they bring about public and higher education. There is also strength in numbers; if all adjuncts were on board with a reformation initiative, much progress could be made. These strengths are discussed in the chapter in depth.

NARRATIVE

Adjunct?

Jennifer was pregnant. For the first time. And she was very excited but also very nervous.

Jennifer was actually Dr. Jennifer Wilhite, and she had just graduated three months earlier with her doctorate. Her husband had just switched jobs and was working for an insurance agency as an auditor. It was a good job, but it would take a while before his salary got up to where it had been in his previous job. Jennifer had hoped to find a tenure-track job but was not in a hurry. Now, though, with a baby, they would need another income to make ends meet. With John at a new job, she thought working as an adjunct at her alma mater would be a great solution.

Jennifer had a great experience with State University in her doctoral program. She was involved in the college as a teaching assistant and worked with her faculty advisor on two research projects. She even had a publication from her dissertation research in press. She knew that universities did not "hire their own" for tenure-track positions, but she thought she could work as an adjunct and be involved again.

Jennifer met with Dr. Long, the department chair, for twenty minutes about the possibility of being an adjunct. He said he needed someone to teach the foundations course and he could give her four sections, one face to face and three online. Her salary would be $14,000 a semester for four courses. Of course, benefits would come out of that. Her pregnancy was not an issue because she was due at the beginning of May. And she could have a carrel in the graduate assistants' office. Jennifer took it; it was not exactly what she hoped for, but it would work.

Jennifer dealt with the departmental administrative assistant to get books, forms, and all the information she needed about the course she was teaching. She was provided a syllabus and the course requirements. As a teaching assistant, she worked with a faculty advisor who oversaw all the TAs teaching a specific course; as an adjunct she was left on her own. It did not take long to get ready.

After a month working, Jennifer had been on campus exactly four times. Her class met at 4:30 p.m. on Tuesdays, and it was the only time she had to go to campus. Her other sections were online, and she worked on those from her home computer as her belly began to grow. No one had really ever told her how much work it was to teach online. She felt as if the computer were just an extension of her fingers. She looked forward to the Tuesday class.

Around midterm, as her belly became a bump, Jennifer became lonely. She had thought that by working as an adjunct, she would still get to see her professors and have some conversations about how things were going and issues that were in the news. She finally realized she had been replaced by new doctoral candidates.

It was not personal, but the professors had done their job with her, and now they had new students to teach and mentor. She also looked for other adjuncts. Maybe there were some other leftovers from the program still in town, but she found that most had moved on or found positions outside the university. Most of all, she missed the exciting conversations and the exchange of ideas.

By the end of the semester, Jennifer had given up any hope that working as an adjunct would be rewarding or stimulating. She was on campus once a week and saw only her students. Her only communication with the department was through the administrative assistant. She was teaching four classes and did not have time to work on any more manuscripts from her dissertation. More than anything, she was confused. Was this all academia had to offer?

Resolved to the ostracism of adjuncts, Jennifer began her spring semester. By now she could feel the baby kick and turn. She began looking forward to the birth of their first daughter. Her focus homed in more on the pregnancy and less on the work.

One afternoon she went to campus early to make copies of a last-minute article she wanted to share with the class. After she left the workroom she realized she had a while before class, so she decided to sit outside and read. Shortly, she heard someone else come out to the courtyard. She looked up and saw her faculty advisor lighting a pipe. He saw her and walked over.

"Hi, Jennifer. I heard you were teaching the foundations class. How's it going?" Dr. Timpson asked.

"Well, it's okay. Just not what I was expecting," Jennifer replied.

Dr. Timpson sat down as his pipe went out. "What were you expecting?" he asked.

"I don't know. I guess I thought it would more like my program. It's just really lonely and unchallenging. I am beginning to doubt my decision about becoming a professor," Jennifer said.

Dr. Timpson actually laughed. "Jennifer, academia is nothing like teaching as an adjunct. Hang in there and get a tenure-track position, and you will be great. You are one of the best students I have ever had," he said.

Jennifer furrowed her brow, deciding whether she should believe him or not.

"You will be a great professor and a great mom," Dr. Timpson said as he emptied his pipe and went back into the building.

Jennifer marked her place in her book with her finger and thought. In a minute, she decided to trust Dr. Timpson. This semester she would give her best to her students and send out applications and letters while watching her belly grow.

Maybe by the time the baby came, she would be on her way.

NARRATIVE

Breaking into the Academy

Dr. Smith spent five years working on his doctoral studies and writing his dissertation. He had worked his way through undergraduate college by working for a tutoring service. Then he worked as a calculus teacher while he earned his master's and doctorate. Dr. Smith was thirty-four years old. He was excited to be called Dr. Smith and had started sending out applications and cover letters as soon as he had defended his dissertation. It was now April, and he had no offers.

Dr. Smith was married to Nancy, who taught English at the local high school. Nancy and Dr. Smith had two twin boys who were three years old. Nancy had three brothers and one sister and really wanted a big family. Dr. Smith did, too, but he also wanted a way to support them. He had always heard that the higher your degree, the higher your salary. He was counting on the doctorate degree to make them financially stable. After all, two teacher salaries weren't going to provide for a family of six or eight.

Dr. Smith was not really worried until July rolled around. He had gone on a few interviews but still had not received an offer. Luckily, he had not resigned from the high school yet. His wife was happy to still work with him, and each day she reassured him and hinted at another baby.

It was late August and the high school had resumed classes when the department chair from a university sixty miles away called and asked Dr. Smith to teach as an adjunct for the semester. His class would be on Thursday nights from 6:00 to 9:00. Dr. Smith, thinking this was his chance, accepted the offer.

Two years later, Dr. Smith was still teaching high school and adjuncting at two different institutions. Nancy really wanted a baby, and the boys were in kindergarten. If Dr. Smith wanted a tenure-track position, he'd better get on it.

Dr. Smith had never really given up. He still sent out letters and CVs every month. He was getting tired of the travel in working as an adjunct, as was Nancy. Luckily, in May he was offered a position four states away as a visiting professor. Again, Dr. Smith, thinking it was his big chance, accepted the offer.

The family moved, and Dr. Smith tried to adjust to the new campus and to higher education in general. The department chair said that all he had to do was keep up the good work and interview in the spring and the tenure-track position was his. Dr. Smith and Nancy were very excited and started talking about having another baby.

In the spring, the search committee was named, and the chair was a colleague Dr. Smith had somehow irritated. He was interviewed, and the position was not filled. Devastated, Dr. Smith began to question his future in higher education. What was he doing wrong? How do other people get positions? Should he work on his networking skills?

Not knowing what else to do, Dr. Smith started applying for calculus positions at local high schools. Out of the blue, a call came from a southern school in a state close to his home state, and they wanted to interview him.

Dr. Smith did not get his hopes up, but he decided to give it one more try. Eight years after starting his doctoral work and three years and two moves after graduating, Dr. Smith got his tenure-track position. And a baby.

OBSTACLES TO EDUCATIONAL REFORM

Undergraduate Course Load

One of the major obstacles to education reform for this perspective is the undergraduate course load of adjuncts. In many large institutions, adjuncts or teaching assistants teach the introductory and foundations courses for the undergraduate students. Adjunct faculty members in these courses can be very effective teaching the introductory and foundational content to undergraduates. The challenge to the teacher preparation programs using adjunct faculty members for these courses is the focus on preparing preservice teachers to be effective change agents in their future schools.

Teacher preparation programs are already finding it difficult to integrate a strand of change theory and educational reform into the teacher education curriculum. What new teachers need to know is immense. In order to survive, much less thrive, in the first years of teaching, the preservice teacher needs to understand curriculum, learning theory, instructional and assessment methods, classroom management, diversity issues, educational law, and so much more. Asking tenure-track faculty members to also teach how to be an effective change agent or even trying to nurture a disposition to educational reform is difficult.

Adjunct teachers are given a syllabus and a book and the goals for the course and are expected to prepare the preservice teacher to add to the foundation they learn in those classes. Having them also address the dispositions toward education reform or change agency is unfair to the adjunct faculty member. Her time and resources are limited, and typically the support from the department is limited, as depicted in the earlier narrative.

The argument is not a call for the exclusion of adjuncts from teaching undergraduate courses but a call for analyzing and reflecting on the best place for adjuncts and the need for different support systems for those instructors. The reality is that universities need adjunct faculty members in order to function. It is then the responsibility of deans and department chairs to make sure the adjunct instructor is utilized in the most effective and responsible way not only for the programs but also out of respect for and appreciation of the adjunct instructor. For educational reform to occur, the role of the adjunct instructor will need to be adjusted and then supported within colleges of education.

Lack of Opportunities

Adjunct faculty members are usually limited to very specific courses. Department chairs evaluate courses and decide which ones could be taught by adjuncts and which need to be taught by tenure-track faculty. This leads to limited opportunities for the adjunct faculty member.

As a new tenure-track faculty member, one is introduced to the program and given courses that fit one's scope of expertise and then mentored through other opportunities, including new courses, grant work, and research projects. Grant work could lead to development of a new course or program. Research could change the way a course is taught. Retirements and resignations could mix up the courses among faculty members. Basically, there is opportunity for growth and change in the life of a tenure-track faculty member. However, these opportunities are not available to the adjunct faculty member.

Professors who work as adjuncts still grow and develop, but it is under their own discretion. The department is not there to guide them to professional development that aligns with the mission or vision of the department. This lack of connection makes it difficult for adjunct faculty members to act as change agents or even support change in the departments. By overlooking adjunct faculty development, the teacher preparation programs are undermining any change they are trying to undertake.

Disconnection from Faculty

Another major obstacle is the disconnection from faculty members. As discussed earlier, the adjunct faculty member is restricted to certain courses to teach and has limited support for professional development. Adjunct faculty members are also separated from the traditional faculty. Activities that bring the faculty membership of a college together oftentimes overlook the adjuncts.

Adjunct faculty members are not held to the same standards for research and service as tenure-track faculty. At first glance, this makes sense. They are on a semester-by-semester contract with no option of tenure. Working on research and service are not included in the adjunct contract and could possibly interfere with the teaching responsibilities if the loads are high. However, by not including adjunct faculty members in research and service with tenure-track faculty, a chasm forms between the two groups. In the academy, professors are brought together through college and university service.

Conversations happen between colleagues that may have never crossed paths had it not been for service work. The same is true in research. Two colleagues may come together to work on a project based on different areas of expertise but would not have joined together if their only responsibility was teaching. These aspects of higher education naturally allow for collaboration and conversation. The adjuncts, by missing out on these ingrained opportunities, become even more disconnected from the faculty and departments and in turn from any innovations or initiatives being implemented.

Undervalued: Pay and Load

As if the previous obstacles were not enough to disenfranchise the adjunct faculty from any educational reform, they are also undervalued in terms of compensation and course load. Adjuncts earn significantly less than tenure-track faculty and often teach higher loads.

According to Jaschik (2011), adjuncts teaching a full load in Pennsylvania would be eligible for public assistance on a $25,000 salary. Typically, adjuncts can expect around $3,000 per course with no guarantee of work in the next semester. So a full-time adjunct could teach four preps at $3,000 apiece for four months. That breaks down to $18.75 an hour. An assistant professor makes on average $66,564 a year. Based on a four/four load, that breaks down to $52.00 an hour. The assistant professor is also responsible for research and service, but many times the assistant professor and the adjunct professor start out on equal footing with the same degrees and dissertations. The problem here is that the pay discrepancy will eventually dent the morale of the adjunct faculty member, and that in turn leads to an unwillingness to participate in reform that goes beyond the basic teaching requirements.

In addition, the adjunct may be required to teach more courses than the tenure-track faculty in order to make a full load. It is understandable in that tenure-track faculty members are also responsible for service and research. A lighter teaching load allows for the time necessary for research development and service time requirements. The high teaching load for adjuncts may come at the price of faster burnout. Teaching four preps each semester for a smaller salary than a tenure-track position will lead to frustration and exhaustion. In these conditions, it is easy to see why this perspective can hinder educational initiatives from the teacher preparation programs.

STRENGTHS OF THIS PERSPECTIVE

On the other hand, this perspective offers two really important strengths. Many adjuncts have a more realistic view on education. These views should be capitalized on. Also, there is strength in numbers. The adjunct pool is growing in times of budget cuts and economic hardships. Movement toward change could use these numbers.

Realistic Views of Education

The adjunct population may have more realistic views of the public education system than some tenured faculty members. It is especially common in teacher education that doctoral students come out of the public education system as teachers. Their views of education may be more realistic and definitely more up to date than the professor who has been in the university a number of years. As the narrative previously described, many new doctoral graduates take adjunct positions as a way of entry into a teacher education program. The fact that they are more recent graduates implies their experiences in public education are more recent.

There is another reason that these professors may have a more realistic view of education, and that is the tendency for teacher education programs to assign adjuncts to introductory courses and supervisory courses. Many programs have field-based experiences in the early course sequence to introduce prospective preservice teachers to the PK–12 classroom through the eyes of a teacher rather than a student. Adjuncts who are responsible for those courses are also responsible for the supervision of the field component. The adjunct instructor is privy to conversations and concerns of the preservice teacher about the schools.

In addition, she will communicate with the schools about the candidates and the placements. By the daily or weekly entry into the public school, the adjunct instructor gains insight into systems, policies, and challenges that the schools face regularly. This is the biggest strength of this perspective. Unfortunately, adjunct faculty members are rarely called upon to share this rich information they have accumulated over the semesters.

Strength in Numbers

It is estimated that over half of college courses are taught by part-time faculty (McArdle, 2006), and, as the saying goes, there is strength in numbers. The use of adjunct faculty has been a national conversation in the past few years. What should the balance be between adjunct and tenure-track faculty? Is there a tipping point? In today's economy, are there other alternatives? Why get a doctoral degree when there is no guarantee of a tenure-track position?

Despite all the talk, the number of adjunct faculty members has risen over the past few decades. In relation to educational change, the growth makes it necessary to include the group in the change process.

When thinking about educational reform, the adjunct group is probably not considered a major stakeholder, but if the numbers of adjuncts maintain their current level or continue to increase, they will not be able to be ignored. The adjunct group has the numbers to sustain effective educational reform. If there is a movement toward an innovation and there is buy-in from the adjunct population, the innovation has a good chance of success. Unfortunately, this adjunct group is left out due to turnover, low pay, high course loads, and many other factors. Instead of looking at adjunct faculty as a stopgap measure to make do until a tenure-track line can be secured, educator preparation programs need to look at them as stakeholders and resources for data, information, and support.

MOVING FORWARD

The potential for influence from this perspective is great. Resources and support are needed though, in order to access their influence. By working toward mentoring programs for adjunct faculty, inviting adjuncts to the table on change, and facilitating professional development, teacher education programs could develop a great resource for educational reform.

Mentoring Adjuncts

Mentoring of educational professionals has been a constant theme in this book so far. Adjunct faculty, like previous perspectives, need to have consistent and effective mentoring in order to be effective teacher educators. Additionally, this mentoring is critical for educational reform. Traditionally, the adjunct faculty has been a disenfranchised group of educators functioning autonomously with little oversight or interference. In actuality, they have not been treated as professionals, much less as stakeholders.

A consistent mentoring program matching adjuncts to tenure-track faculty members can help the communication and discussion of issues related to courses, curriculum, and eventually reform. There is a difference between a mentoring program and supervision. Adjunct faculty members need the same professional mentoring as any other faculty member. Gone is the time that an adjunct was teaching for pleasure, and now is the time of the future tenure-track faculty trying to make a way into the academy. Teacher educator programs need to accept the new professional adjunct and provide the necessary mentoring and support not only for immediate success but for long-term success in teacher education.

Bring Them to the Table

Along with mentoring, educator preparation programs need to invite adjuncts to participate in the conversation. This perspective is perpetually overlooked as a resource in educational reform, and that must be rectified. Colleges of education are great at inviting teachers, principals, school board members, and peers to give insights and ideas to meet challenges, but adjuncts are rarely asked for an opinion. This perspective is a stakeholder and does have a vested interest in the future of teacher education.

In order to have the adjunct faculty member become a part of the conversation and solution, there needs to be an adjustment in the relationship between adjunct faculty members and the tenure-track professors. Including adjunct faculty in more traditional tenure-track roles can help facilitate the development of a new relationship. By serving on committees, adjunct faculty begin to understand the demands on tenure-track faculty, and in turn, the tenure-track faculty begin to understand the great benefit of another professional perspective. By supporting collaborative research, the same outcomes can be achieved. The major challenge is to begin to respect the perspective and utilize the information available from the adjuncts.

Facilitate Professional Development

Professional development has become another theme of this book. This perspective also needs tailored professional development. More and more often, the adjunct instructor is a PhD looking for a tenure-track position. Due to the constraints of the role as adjunct, the professional development of such a scholar can stagnate. It is in the best interest of the future of teacher education to provide and facilitate appropriate professional development for the adjunct faculty. If left to their own limited resources, professional development may be overlooked.

One may see this argument for the evolution of the adjunct position as an argument for treating them as tenure-track faculty. Obviously, teacher education programs cannot support adjunct faculty with time and money in the same way as they support tenure-track faculty. Tenure-track faculties are held to certain requirements that adjuncts are not. However, in the best possible world, that current adjunct is a future tenure-track professor, and if not supported and challenged, she will not enter the academy with the necessary skills.

Therefore, a tailored, very specific type of professional development for adjuncts is needed. Educator preparation programs can provide book studies, workshops, and webinars for adjunct faculty. Study groups or research support groups are another possibility for professional development. Any way to keep the adjunct faculty member engaged and learning will be worth the payoff later.

CONCLUSIONS

The adjunct perspective holds a great deal of potential for supporting and sustaining educational reform. Adjuncts bring strength in numbers and a unique perspective of the realities of the public school. The challenge is how teacher preparation programs utilize their expertise in the course sequence, the lack of opportunities, and disconnection from faculty as well as a high teaching load and low pay. However, these challenges may be overcome by listening to the ideas of this perspective, by mentoring them through their professional life, and by providing opportunities for growth. It is possible for this perspective to be the most influential in educational reform.

REFERENCES

Jaschik, S. (2011). Documenting adjuncts' pay gap. Retrieved from http://www.insidehighered.com/news/2011/01/20study_documents_pay_gap_faced_by_adjuncts

McArdle, E. (2006). The adjunct explosion. Retrieved from http://universitybusiness.ccsct.com/page.cfm?p=159

Chapter Six

Tenure-Track Assistant Professor

The tenure-track assistant professor is a position that demands productivity within a specific time frame. Within six years an assistant professor is expected to show proficiency and excellence in teaching, scholarship, and service. The pressures are tremendous. The pressures and expectations of the tenure-track assistant professor are what make this perspective different from others. It also makes the obstacles and challenges unique.

The narratives in this chapter discuss the issues of power connected to the position of a tenure-track assistant professor and how turnover can affect the role of the assistant professor. The second narrative focuses on the process of tenure and promotion and its relationship to reform.

Obstacles to education reform related to this perspective include the process of tenure and promotion and the time frame and time demands of the position. In today's changing higher education environment, there is more and more emphasis on accountability, and this can be a challenge for a new professor. The last challenge for this perspective is the lack of power as junior faculty. All of these elements can create a climate where educational reform is the least of many priorities.

It is interesting that one of the obstacles of this group is also one of the benefits. The tenure and promotion process requires certain products for success, and these can be beneficial to creating change in education. This perspective is like the new teacher in that there is an idealism and eagerness that can be tapped. Finally, there is a preparedness from the doctoral programs to make change and act as a change agent.

Many of the ways to move this group forward into action are the same as previous groups. The process of tenure and promotion should be revisited to act as a catalyst or at least a support system of change. This perspective also needs appropriate professional development for growth as well as early and continued connection to schools.

NARRATIVE

Veteran at Three Years?

Dr. Landrum was very excited to have her first tenure-track position. Many of her friends were still looking for positions and working as adjuncts. She felt lucky to be a part of the education faculty at this regional institution. The university had a strong history of teacher education, and she felt included most of the time. Dr. Landrum was part of an eight-member program faculty when she was hired two years ago. She was about to begin her fourth year, and the makeup had changed.

After her first year, one faculty member retired, one moved to a different institution, and one moved to another institution in administration. Three new people were hired. After her second year, one faculty member retired, and one moved with her husband. Two new people were hired.

At the end of her third year, one faculty member resigned for an outside position and the line was not renewed, and one visiting position ended. No new people were hired. At the beginning of her fourth year, she was the veteran faculty member. And she didn't have tenure yet.

During the summer prior to the start of her fourth year, the chair asked her to come in for a talk. Dr. Landrum guessed the meeting might be about the vacant program coordinator position, and she was correct. The chair explained there was no one else to take on the role of program coordinator and that Dr. Landrum had the most experience with the program. She would have a course release for the fall and spring. Dr. Landrum was a little nervous, but she wanted to have a great program and she said yes.

During her first semester as program coordinator, things went fairly smoothly. She worked with the chair on the schedule and made charts of enrollment numbers and projections for the future. It wasn't until November when the dean asked to see the chair and Dr. Landrum that she felt the pressure.

The meeting was brief, but the message was clear: there were too many criticisms of the program from students, alumni, and school districts. Address the issues and make changes. Still, even under some pressure, Dr. Landrum felt optimistic; this was a chance to make a change to make things better.

In the spring semester, Dr. Landrum led the now six-member faculty through program revisions. Some changes were made, and more work was slated for the fall semester. In the meantime, another faculty member had resigned, and Dr. Landrum would chair that search. Summer flew by.

That fall, the pressure began to build. Dr. Landrum was still working on program revisions, but now suddenly people began asking for more. The test scores for certification were too low. What was the action plan? There were too many student teachers with classroom management issues. Where were the revisions for that class? We are going up for NCATE. Will you serve on that committee? Subtly, the work shifted from academics to administrivia. How had this happened?

In April, Dr. Landrum finally cracked. Too many people were asking for too much help. It wasn't their fault; the university was understaffed and everyone was answering to the accountabilities. After a university-wide meeting about accreditation by SACS, Dr. Landrum went back to her office and cried. The system had finally won. In the morning she sent an e-mail resigning the position of program coordinator.

Dr. Landrum had hopes and dreams of making a difference and making changes. She wanted to be one of the ones to change the system, but she could not seem to make any difference as long as she was part of the system. She left the administration of the university to others. She went back to her office, shut her door, and did the work of the academic, and only the work of the academic.

NARRATIVE

Pressures of the Academy

Bryan Harris had just finished his third-year review for tenure. He had two and a half years to prove he was worthy of tenure and promotion at his university. His dean had indicated he was on track for tenure and promotion, but if he did not have at least two more publications he may not make it. The dean also stressed that the university was really moving toward a more research-focused agenda and a grant would almost certainly ensure a positive outcome.

Bryan sighed as he sank down on a bench outside of the building. His wife had just started her doctoral work, and their daughter was about to be driving. His father had just died; and his mom was now living with them. Home was stressful enough without the pressures of work. Days like today made his shoulders sink and his breath come heavy. It was almost too much for one man.

Bryan stood up and stretched his arms, pushed up his glasses, and loosened his tie as he began to walk back to the four-story building that housed his office. He began to plan. He had one presentation from a national conference that needed to be submitted for publication and another paper he was second author on under review. He could edit the presentation paper fairly quickly and have it submitted by the end of the semester.

He needed one more good piece to make sure he was ready. He was currently working on a research project around the role of the teacher educator in development of preservice teachers' teacher identity. He was ready to submit that for presentation and could have it submitted to a journal in a year. Bryan sighed a breath of relief. He could just do it.

The farther he walked, the more he thought about getting a grant. He might be able to do that. His background was science education, and he was sure there was money for STEM education available somewhere. Bryan decided to talk with his chair when he got back to the office.

Bryan didn't even have time to look for Dr. Mosby; she approached him as soon as he stepped off the elevator.

"Oh, Bryan. I have been looking for you. Do you have a few minutes to chat?" she asked.

"Of course," he answered as he followed her into her corner office. She gestured to a seat as she shut the door.

"Great. I hope your review went well." Bryan nodded. "I just need to talk with you about this new initiative from the state related to teacher education."

"What's going on?" Bryan asked.

"Well, the state is developing a new testing system for the secondary schools and have asked teacher education programs to participate in some committee work, and I thought you may be interested in that," she said.

Bryan was interested; he was very interested. He realized he was nodding and sitting forward waiting to hear more. This was just the kind of opportunity for change that he had been hoping to work on.

"I am very interested. What would be involved?" he asked.

"Well, there would be monthly meetings at the state capital and some writing involved. It would take a significant time commitment and I cannot offer you any course releases, but I may be able to help with travel," she said.

"How long does the committee last?" Bryan asked.

"It would be a three-year commitment," Dr. Mosby said.

Bryan suddenly deflated. There was no way he could balance a state committee with tenure and promotion requirements and his family responsibilities. He knew the work would count toward his service, but it would detract from his research. At this point in his life and career, he could not jeopardize his chances for tenure and promotion in the least bit.

"I am sorry, Dr. Mosby. I think I will have to pass this time," Bryan said as he rubbed his eyes.

"Oh, okay. I will find someone else. Thanks, Bryan," Dr. Mosby said, not looking as happy as she did earlier.

Bryan found himself even more deflated than before. How could he ever manage to make any kind of significant change to the profession if he were having to jump through the T&P hoops? Would this pressure ever end? Bryan wondered how this profession had ever sounded appealing.

OBSTACLES TO EDUCATIONAL REFORM

This perspective encounters many obstacles to sustained educational reform. The first obstacle is the tenure and promotion process, but interestingly, this process could also be a strength and will be discussed later as such. In addition, the tenure-track assistant professor must also overcome the challenges of time, the new standards of accountability, and the impotence of junior faculty status in order to make any lasting change.

Tenure and Promotion

The tenure and promotion process is antiquated and moored in issues of years past. However, the current tenure-track assistant professor must still navigate his or her way through the system in order to become a member of the academy.

The original "Statement of Principles on Academic Freedom and Tenure" was produced by the American Association of University Professors and the Association of American Colleges (now Association of American Colleges and Universities) in 1940. The document was revised in 1970 with interpretative comments, and gender-specific language was removed in 1990. In essence, the statement has not changed dramatically in over seventy years.

The statement was and is an important document for higher education. It sets out a standard of practice for the academy. Professors must be protected so that they can teach and discuss controversial issues and challenge the system. The process of tenure is there to ensure that a tenure-track professor is not removed without cause. In other words, a university cannot fire a professor for not spouting the current popular opinions. We have academic freedom and with that a responsibility. The statement sets that process.

The issue is how we as a profession have lost sight of our roles as forward thinkers and groundbreakers and have become caught up in the fear of loss of job security. Tenure is to ensure that professors who challenge the status quo will not suffer repercussions. Today many tenure-track assistant professors have overlooked their ethical and professional responsibility to challenge the status quo in favor of meeting the requirements of job security. As a profession, what is more important?

In addition, the process has become a high-stakes game for the new professor. Departments and colleges set a bar, and the tenure-track assistant professor has a race against a clock to meet the requirements. Do we as a profession need a probationary period for professors? Yes. It makes sense to give new professors a chance to prove they can contribute to the knowledge base in their content. The problem is that the stress of the process makes the process the focus instead of the profession.

The new assistant professor in the narrative had to choose between gaining tenure and enhancing his profession. Demands of tenure and promotion are creating a win-lose situation for the profession at times. There are tenure-track assistant professors who make their research and service agendas align with the needs of the profession, but usually this takes mentoring and collaboration. Why not look at the process of tenure and promotion to see how it can work for not only the universities but also the professor and the profession?

Time

For the tenure-track assistant professor, the demands on time are extreme. A new professor is experiencing new courses and new committee responsibilities and developing a research agenda. As a novice in the academy, finding balance is difficult. Time has been a concern for new faculty members for several years (Carlson, 2008).

A new tenure-track assistant professor faces many challenges in her first position. Even with adjunct or teaching assistant experience, the acculturation to higher education can be difficult. A faculty member is expected to manage twelve hours of courses that include course development, assignment management, grading, book selection, remediation of students, lecture and instructional planning, student conferences, and grade assignments. All of these demand some knowledge of the culture of the department. Are students used to submitting work online? Are midsemester grades required? Do I have freedom to choose any book? How much money are students accustomed to spending on books per class?

Service also demands a significant amount of time. Most tenure-track assistant professors will accept any committee work because they know service is required for tenure. These committees at the college and university level require regular amounts of time from the workday for meetings. On top of that, there is regional, state, and national service, which could demand travel away from campus. How much time is too much to be spending on service? Can I miss class for a state meeting? Which is most important?

Finally, for a successful research agenda, time must be spent planning and conducting research, and significant amounts of time are tied up in writing and editing for publication. When is it appropriate to conduct research? Can I miss office hours to conduct observations? How can I fund this project? How many publications are expected of me each year?

Most tenure-track assistant professors are left to their own devices to create a balanced workweek addressing the needs of all three areas. Little mentoring or instruction is given on how to manage the demands of the professorship. It is understandable to expect a new professor to manage his own academic life; success will mean promotion and tenure. On the other hand, if the world of education is going to make significant changes toward better opportunities for all children, then the assistant professors will have to play a part in that change, and they will need support and guidance to manage the demands of tenure and promotion and educational reform.

Accountability

Higher education today is not the same as it was ten or twenty years ago. The accountability movement that began in public schools with No Child Left Behind (2001) has now begun to move into higher education. Teacher education accreditation has become more rigorous through the National Council for Accreditation of Teacher Education (NCATE) and will likely become even more rigorous as the Council for the Accreditation of Educator Preparation (CAEP) takes over teacher preparation accreditation. In addition, program accreditation for content areas is also moving to continuous improvement based on data-driven decision making. This trend toward higher accountability adds responsibilities to the professors in higher education.

Most teacher preparation programs are aware of the higher standards of accountability nationally and at the state levels. States and accrediting bodies are asking for evidence of data-driven decision making. In order to manage the amount of data it takes to support data-based decision making, many programs are using commercial vendors to digitally manage the data. For the tenure-track assistant professor, this translates into an additional software system that she needs to utilize.

In today's world, the assistant professor is already likely using the everyday word-processing tools and spreadsheets and university e-mail systems and online learning platforms. Accountability is requiring knowledge of another system for data maintenance. In addition, the tenure-track assistant professor must make sure the required assessment is included, assessed, and recorded for program evaluation. This added responsibility also requires time to implement that may take away from time that could be given to educational reform.

Junior Faculty

The last challenge for tenure-track assistant professors is inherent to the position. Tenure-track assistant professors are considered junior faculty. In many departments and universities, the junior faculty status binds the hands of the assistant professor. In order to implement or lead any change initiatives, tenure-track assistant professors must overcome the impotency of the junior faculty status.

The tenure process allows for a probationary period for the assistant professor to establish himself as an academic, and in theory this is a very important time period and protection for the assistant professor. However, the well-intentioned protection for the young faculty member allows limits to the power to initiate change in many instances. Senior faculty in programs may not listen to the junior faculty due only to their novice status in the program.

Additionally, professors across campus may not entertain innovations from untenured faculty due to their junior faculty status. Many times the junior faculty members are not appointed to leadership or to high-profile positions because speaking out and challenging the status quo could be unfavorable to their tenure process. However, by protecting this population to the point of impotency, the profession loses new and innovative ideas from a creative and critical population.

STRENGTHS OF THIS PERSPECTIVE

This perspective also has strengths to help initiate educational reform. One of the biggest obstacles, tenure and promotion, can also be parlayed into a strength for the assistant professor. Additionally, a critical perspective and preparedness for change are significant strengths.

Tenure and Promotion

Tenure and promotion may be obstacles for educational reform for this perspective due to the amount of time and pressure the process entails, but there is possibility to leverage this obstacle into strength. Every tenure-track assistant professor is expected to teach classes, to conduct research, and to provide service to the profession. These are requirements for entry into the academy. It is possible to use these very requirements as a means to educational reform.

First, as discussed in previous chapters, teacher preparation programs must begin to prepare classroom teachers to be change agents upon entering the profession. This movement can align with having teacher education professors think of teaching in terms of agency preparation. Instead of maintaining the traditional teacher preparation curriculum, programs and chairs need to support assistant professors in teaching new teachers how to initiate change and participate in the change process. Instantly, educational reform becomes part of the tenure process through the teaching strand.

In terms of service, new assistant professors need to be matched to service opportunities that afford them the experience of work with schools and classroom teachers. By serving with PK–12 partners, the new faculty members are able to understand what is happening in the public school classrooms more clearly. Working closely with schools allows for assistant professors to discuss and identify the needs of the districts the preservice teachers will be working in as well as meet the tenure requirements for service.

Finally, research agendas need to be aligned to meet the requirements of tenure and promotion and to improve the education profession. This can be easily accomplished not by dictating research agendas but by offering research incentives such as funding and use of graduate students for innovative research. New faculty members could receive a course release if their research agenda met the criteria to be identified as reformative.

By coalescing the process of tenure and promotion and the need for educational reform, the professoriate could protect the new colleague and at the same time empower her to make changes for improvement in educating all children.

Fresh Eyes

Tenure-track assistant professors are able to look at program and university policies and procedures with fresh analytic eyes. As a faculty grows in experience and years served, their ability to step outside the norms of their universities, colleges, and programs is diminished. The assistant professors are more agile at looking critically at practices and asking if there is a more effective way to achieve the same outcome. Working as a professor in any institution of higher education demands time on committees, time teaching, and time writing. Balancing these demands is difficult, and as balance is finally achieved, there may be little incentive to change the process that took so long to perfect.

Veteran professors and administrators need to draw on the fresh eyes of the new assistant professors for constructive criticisms and outside-the-box thinking.

Preparedness

The process of tenure with a probationary period is for the benefit and protection of the new assistant professor, but sometimes the new assistant professor comes from a doctoral program that has prepared him to be a change agent as soon he enters the university. Chairs and administrators need to be able to protect their assistant professors and encourage participation and action from them as well.

In order for significant change to occur in today's educational landscape, all participants must be involved. The doctoral faculty must prepare the future teacher educators to be able to engage in discussion and movements of educational reform. In turn, the universities must be willing to overcome the traditional roles of junior faculty and trust that their colleagues have prepared

change agents for the teacher preparation programs. All the academic preparation of future assistant professors will be wasted if the traditional model of
entrance in to the academy is maintained.

MOVING FORWARD

This perspective has a great deal of potential for educational reform. The
assistant professor's sphere of influence can be wide and can encompass
many different types of educational professionals. The assistant professor
will prepare the preservice teacher, will advance the knowledge base through
research, and will eventually be the full professor who educates the future
assistant professors. By revisiting tenure and promotion, mentoring this
group, making connections to schools early, and facilitating professional
development, the profession can make sure these men and women are successful.

Revisit Tenure and Promotion

Tenure and promotion have a definite and foundational place in the academy.
The processes are in place for the benefit of the faculty and the integrity of
the colleges. There is no argument that a probationary period of acclimation
to higher education is valuable, but the pressures and high-stakes mentalities
of some colleges and universities are undermining the benefits to the process.

As a profession of professors, higher education needs to look at the role of
tenure and promotion. Gaining tenure need not be the equivalent of high-
stakes testing in America's high schools. The process needs to be refined to
support new faculty and protect them while at the same time empowering
them to make contributions to the change movement. If assistant professors
are bound from challenging the status quo until tenure and promotion have
been attained, then little will change. In the next chapter, the role of the
tenured faculty member will be discussed. Many times this perspective opts
out after seven years of stress and unending work.

Mentoring New Faculty

Empowering assistant professors will take mentoring. The research on mentoring new faculty is comprehensive. Structured mentoring may not be the
most effective approach; a more organic approach tends to work better. Mentoring relationships that tend to happen naturally may be the most effective
forms of mentoring. In this instance, it is not the how of the mentoring
program but the ultimate goal that is of concern.

Mentoring of new faculty members should include social, political, personal, academic, and scholarly approaches. Many programs assign a mentor

faculty member to a new assistant professor and expect that one person to guide and answer questions about policies, procedures, publishing, teaching, service, finances, family, and more. A more holistic approach may be to have a mentoring fellowship, where faculty members are available as experts in one of the areas. The need is for all those areas to be addressed in some way.

For example, a new assistant professor begins a new year with a great research agenda, classroom experience, and assignment to a university committee. At home, though, she has two preschoolers and no ideas for child care. Her productivity will not be the same in teaching, research, and scholarship if she is worried about her children compared to having a colleague offer suggestions and advise on how to balance family, work, and day care.

New assistant professors need to be mentored as a whole person rather than as an author, teacher, or committee member. A more comprehensive mentoring approach will result in a more engaged and active faculty member in teaching, research, and service as well as educational reform.

Connect to Schools Early and Mentor Liaisons

To reap the benefits of the tenure-track assistant professor perspective, the assistant professor needs to be connected to a public school early and mentored in the ways to work with partner schools. Schools are the center point for all teacher preparation programs; professors of education cannot exist without public schools. Many times, universities send clinical faculty or adjuncts to work with the public schools. These professionals may be great with their schools, but typically there will be a disconnection to the program. By putting the assistant professor in the field, the connection between the public school and the university program is strengthened.

Connecting assistant professors to schools early is important, but it cannot be done without support from the administration of the university and the public schools. In the university setting, the department or college is responsible for providing training and support to the assistant professor who is working in the field. Most doctoral programs are not preparing future teacher educators in how to work with an institutional partner. It is then the responsibility of their new academic home to help acclimate them to the process of partnerships.

Facilitate Professional Development

Academics is one of the few professions that leave professional development up to the individual. Professors may attend conferences of their choice and then attend sessions they think will be interesting. Some professors may attend one conference a year, some none, and others more than four. Many professors are constrained by financial support. Some universities will pay for a conference only if the professor is presenting, and some offer no support at all. Professional development works, and a more focused approach would be useful for assistant professors.

There are several ways to support the professional growth of the assistant professor. One is financial support. All assistant professors could be financially supported to attend a relevant conference in relation to educational change. If money is not available, colleges and departments could develop in-house professional development opportunities for all new assistant professors. Workshops could focus on change, diversity, publishing, and more. Another way to work professional development into the lives of the assistant professors is by collaborating between universities to provide online modules or webinars. The possibilities are endless, but the bottom line is that tenure-track assistant professors need more support if they are expected to engage in the educational reform movement.

CONCLUSIONS

In conclusion, this perspective brings a lot of obstacles that will hinder any attempt to implement educational reform, but it also brings a great deal of potential. To become an effective change agent, the assistant professor must overcome the tenure and promotion process, the demands on time, the new demands of accountability, and the impotency of the status of junior faculty. These can be overcome by drawing on the strengths of the tenure and promotion policy, the assistant professors' fresh eyes, and their preparedness from the doctoral program. To support the tenure-track assistant professor, teacher preparation programs should revisit the role and expectation of tenure and promotion, connect the assistant professor to a school early and with support, and also provide effective and relevant professional development.

REFERENCES

American Association of University Professors. (2011). 1940 Statement of Principles on Academic Freedom and Tenure. Retrieved from http://www.aaup.org/NR/rdonlyres/EBB1B330-33D3-4A51-B534-CEE0C7A90DAB/0/1940StatementofPrinciplesonAcademicFreedomandTenure.pdf

Carlson, J. A. (2008). If I had only known: Challenges experienced by women new to the professoriate. *Advancing Women in Leadership Journal* 28. Retrieved from http://advancingwomen.com/awl/awl_wordpress/if-i-had-only-known-challenges-experienced-by-women-new-to-the-professoriate/

Chapter Seven

Tenured Faculty

In order for any educational reform to take place and be sustained, all perspectives addressed in this book must be on board. Yet it is the tenured faculty member who is unique. This group actually has some power to initiate change on its own. This fact provides an interesting set of obstacles and strengths for this group.

The narratives in this chapter look at the tenured professor who, after meeting all the requirements for tenure and promotion, gives up. The associate professor or full professor is so burned out by all the work done in order to establish academic credibility that there is no energy left for educational reform. The second narrative depicts an associate professor who is successful and productive. As chairs and deans take notice, the workload for him increases exponentially to the point that time is scarce and there is no resource for educational reform.

The obstacles are many for this perspective. First, after meeting the high standards for tenure and promotion, the associate professor has a very narrow specific research agenda that he has spent years developing. Closely related to that issue is the concept of expert fields. The associate professor may be an expert in one aspect of curriculum or theory or assessment, and this leads to a comfort zone that is not conducive for change. Also, these faculty members feel connected and possessive of specific courses in the curriculum, which can lead to resistance to change. Finally, these faculty are typically the most disconnected from public schools.

The strengths are unique as well. This perspective has vast experience in educational trends and movements. They are also protected by tenure, which enables them to safely challenge the status quo and question new policies and procedures. Finally, this group has some power intrinsic to their perspective.

To utilize this group, there are several things educator preparation programs can do. Associate professors need to be connected to new faculty as soon as possible for program collaboration and mentoring. This group also needs to be reconnected to public schools in a way that is appropriate for both the school and the professor. Finally, this group also needs continual professional development.

NARRATIVE

Giving Up

After seven years of sixty-hour work weeks, Dr. Miller was tired. He had researched, written, served, graded, lectured, and professored until he was exhausted. At the faculty meeting today, he would be recognized as the newest tenured professor in the department. Waves of relief swept over him, and he was sure his wife was relieved as well. She was tired of hearing him worry and "what if" every day.

Dr. Miller met up with his two colleagues, Dr. Anne Meadows and Dr. Perry Smith, outside the department office. They all had their coffee and started walking toward the lecture hall for the opening faculty meeting of the semester.

Dr. Miller felt oddly depressed. He had been excited about the first day of school since his first day in kindergarten. He loved the endless possibilities of a new year; he loved the new school supplies, fresh syllabi, and calendars. He even had a special tie he wore on the first day every year since his first day of graduate school. But this fall, he was feeling empty and awash.

He was startled back to reality when he heard Anne and Perry laughing. Both were going up for tenure and promotion this year and had a little extra nervous energy. "I said, how does it feel to be Associate Professor Miller now? You with us, John?" Perry asked.

"Oh yeah. I was just thinking about class," Dr. Miller answered.

"Wow. I might slack off a little if I had tenure," Anne joked. Dr. Miller smiled, but somehow it was not that funny.

They had arrived at the lecture hall, and Dr. Meadows and Dr. Smith both mingled with the rest of the faculty, catching up and welcoming all back. Dr. Miller found a seat and saved a couple for his friends.

He had picked up an agenda on the way in and began looking at it. The very first item was "Congratulations on Tenure and Promotion" followed by a list of three faculty members, including himself. Dr. Miller wondered how the other two new associate professors were doing this morning.

Dr. Young sat down beside Dr. Miller. Dr. Young was the chair for his department. "John, I was just thinking of you. I got an RFP on a grant that I think would really work in our department. I think you would be just the person to write and handle this one. Let's talk later," he said, as he stood and moved on to welcoming another faculty member.

Suddenly all the noise faded, and Dr. Miller sat very still. He looked down at his hands in his lap. Even at rest they looked ready to type another sentence or e-mail. He fingered his gold wedding band and his new watch that was a surprise congratulatory gift from his kids. He had missed so much. And for what? What did it matter? Whose life had he changed? What difference had he made? At that moment he could feel the last drop of idealism and hope evaporate from him.

Dr. Miller stood up and waved when the dean called out his name for recognition, and then he sat down. The rest of the meeting passed with little to garner his attention. As it concluded, Dr. Miller had made his decision. He had a job, a job for life even. He could do his job two thousand hours a year. But somewhere in the past seven years, his career had died.

He left the lecture hall and knew he would not write a grant or probably anything else for that matter. He would teach, grade, and meet. He would get a paycheck, but he would not change the world.

NARRATIVE

Getting Too Much

Dr. Hudson was about to begin her fourth year as an associate professor. Since her tenure and promotion, Dr. Hudson had continued to grow as a scholar and leader. She had published a few articles and was on the board of one national association and the editor of a national journal. In her teaching, Dr. Hudson had begun to work with more graduate students and lead thesis committees. Dr. Hudson enjoyed this work immensely. Every day held something new.

Unfortunately, there was some tension in Dr. Hudson's professional life. The dean of the college of education, Dean Honeycutt, and the chair of Dr. Hudson's department, Dr. Sawyer, were both calling on Dr. Hudson more and more frequently. In the past three years, Dr. Hudson had chaired two search committees for the department, chaired the tenure committee, chaired the college diversity committee, served on the university policy committee, and worked on the NCATE accreditation. She did not have a single day without a meeting of some kind.

During her annual review, Dr. Sawyer had lauded her on her outstanding contributions to the college and department. In addition, she got a great review from Dean Honeycutt echoing the chair's same commendations. At the end of the week she had a meeting scheduled with the dean, and she felt it was going to be an invitation for more work and responsibility.

Dr. Hudson did not mind her responsibilities in the college and university, but at times she found those hard to balance with her obligations to her profession on a national level. She struggled with ways to manage her time and her obligations. Where could she cut responsibilities? She felt pulled in many different directions and lost as to which way to go. She was devoted to her college, and she would "bleed orange," as they say. But how much was too much?

Little did Dr. Hudson know that the same issues were a topic of discussion for Dean Honeycutt and Dr. Sawyer. The two met on Tuesday prior to Dr. Hudson's meeting with the dean on Thursday. Dean Honeycutt felt Dr. Hudson was one of the few tenured professors in the college that could take on some more administrative duties and leadership roles. Dr. Sawyer felt the same way but wanted Dr. Hudson to work in the department as an assistant department chair rather than at the dean's level. The argument was well supported on both sides.

Basically, there were too few tenured professors to share all the leadership needs for the departments and colleges. Many of the tenured professors seemed to shut their office doors and do their own thing. Both the dean and the department chair were all too aware that the heavy reliance on a few professors for leadership would lead to early burnout. It was a dangerous game for everyone. Nothing was resolved between the dean and the chair; basically, it would be Dr. Hudson's decision.

On Thursday, Dean Honeycutt laid out the options for Dr. Hudson. She could work more at the college level or more at the department level, but they needed her help somewhere. Dr. Hudson was overwhelmed. She already had obligations and responsibilities that filled up her days and weeks.

How much more could she possibly do? She was distraught. She wanted her college to excel; she was devoted to her university. But what about the projects and work she was doing to make changes nationally? It felt as if she would have to make a choice. She asked the dean for time to think until Monday.

The weekend was difficult and unsettling, but on Monday morning Dr. Hudson went to see the dean. After thinking about many options, Dr. Hudson told the dean she would be happy to serve with the dean or with the department. She wanted to make her college the best college it could be.

Part of Dr. Hudson wondered about her decision to let go of her national opportunities, but at least at home she knew she would see some change and progress, even if it was only in her college.

OBSTACLES TO EDUCATIONAL REFORM

This perspective has unique obstacles that can block the progress of educational reform. Tenured professors have to overcome the time and devotion to their own agendas of research and scholarship. They also have to be willing to step outside their comfort zones in their expert fields and expert courses. Finally, one of the biggest obstacles is overcoming the disconnection between tenured faculty and the public schools.

Focus on Own Agenda

One of the requirements of tenure and promotion is a well-developed research agenda. This research agenda comes with years of development. The assistant professor may bring in research topics from dissertation work and further that work. By the end of the probationary period, most assistant professors have a narrowed research focus that has been developed with many resources, including time and funding. The personal investment is great.

Due to the high personal investment in a research agenda, it easy for the new tenured professor to feel comfortable and established in this particular area. Research areas develop through personal interest and experience, which means that many times the research being conducted has little to do with educational reform. When new reform movements are introduced and need support from tenured faculty, it may challenge the time available due to the professor's desire to work on his own research.

Additionally, many newly tenured faculty members may feel a sense of freedom after meeting the tenure and promotion requirements. A research agenda born out of dissertation research or necessity for publication may fall by the wayside in favor of a more meaningful research focus. For example, a professor in teacher education may have worked on publishing about diversity issues in secondary education for years but would really prefer to pursue research about the longitudinal effects of arts participation on students. The time limits for tenure have limited the longer studies, and now, after meeting the requirements for tenure, the professor has more time to devote to a longitudinal study. These personal preferences may take up the time needed for participation in reformation movements.

Expert Field and Expert Courses

A closely connected issue is the concept of expert fields and expert courses. A professor in teacher education may feel that she is knowledgeable about a single, specific field of knowledge and that she is the best fit to teach specific courses. Both of these may act as obstacles when trying to implement an innovation in teacher education.

In order to make effective changes to the educational system, the education profession needs to be willing to be creative and innovative. As Sarason (1996) talks about, we need to look at the schooling system from an outside viewpoint and challenge the traditions that are ingrained in it. For this to happen, many professionals will need to be able to step out of their comfort zones.

It will be difficult to ask a professor whose specialty is the principalship to think about campuses with only teacher leaders. The academic success and identity for many professors is tied to their expert field. When the profession begins to question the necessity or the tradition of such fields, the professor may feel defensive and under attack. The personal investment makes it hard to create innovative change without damaging the comfort zone of the professor.

Likewise, expert courses can be an obstacle. In higher education, there is territoriality and a teaching hierarchy in many colleges and universities. Many assistant professors are brought in teaching introductory and foundational courses while the tenured, veteran faculty members have the opportunity to teach graduate courses and special topics. Once a professor has worked his way through the ranks and is able to have more freedom in what he is teaching, it becomes more difficult to divorce him from that course.

An example is a program in elementary education that wants to remove the classroom management course from the degree plan and infuse classroom management strategies throughout the program. The faculty member who teaches the current classroom management course and who has written classroom management texts will feel threatened and territorial. She may even say that it is necessary for preservice teachers to have a classroom management course for them to be successful.

The personal investment in that field and in those courses has become an obstacle for reform; the professor will not consider an alternative, innovative structure because her academic identity is so closely tied to that content. These are difficult obstacles to overcome because they deal with personal feelings and opinions. Careful consideration on how to manage these faculty members is critical to educational reform.

Disconnection from Schools

The tenured professor can also be the most disconnected from the public schools. As a professor progresses in his academic career, he is rewarded with more choice in course selection, more graduate work, more research time, and more varied service opportunities. This tends to lead to a higher number of associate and full professors teaching few classes overall and more graduate courses where there is little to do with initial teacher preparation.

Graduate faculty members teach courses that are peripheral to initial teacher preparation. They may teach in endorsement programs such as English as a second language or professional certification programs such as principal and school counselor. These programs may have a field-based component built into the curriculum, but it is usually very specific to the content field. The superintendent professor is not likely to interact with classroom teachers or public school students. This lack of connection leads to a narrow definition of schooling that may be informed by only the previous professional experience of the professor. Constant connection to the public schools is a key to implementing and sustaining any reformation. By overlooking the need for this connection, programs are leaving an obstacle in the way of change.

STRENGTHS OF THIS PERSPECTIVE

As with the obstacles to this perspective, the strengths are also different from the ones discussed in previous chapters. The major strength of this perspective is the immense amount of experience that accompanies these professors. After attaining tenure, they are also protected, to an extent, and can question the policies and practices of the academy. Finally, the tenured professorship holds some intrinsic power due to the professional accomplishments of the position.

Experience

One of the greatest strengths of this perspective is the experience that tenured professors bring to the profession. By the time an academic reaches tenured status, she has had at least six years at the university and possible public school experience. These experiences can prove invaluable to the educational reform movement.

Many teacher education professors have public school experience to draw on as they teach and research in the academy. This experience informs many choices and colors the way they view teacher education and preparation. For example, a former classroom teacher who struggled with classroom management issues may focus heavily on those strategies in the course she teaches as an associate professor. The professors with public school experience also have a sense of how professional development works in public schools and how induction and turnover affect schools and classrooms.

Associate professors and full professors also have the experience of being part of the academy for several years. In this instance, being part of a teacher education program allows for experiences with innovations and reform movements. In other words, these professors have seen a lot of successes and failures in the attempts to bring change to programs. These two types of experiences can be helpful for future reform efforts.

Safety to Challenge

By having been granted tenure, the associate and full professors are afforded protection from political fallout. A tenured professor can question and challenge decisions in the college or university without fear of political repercussions that may be levied on an untenured professor. By no means is it right or ethical to withhold tenure or derail an assistant professor's career based solely on the fact that he was willing to dissent from the popular position, but it does happen and is a real concern for the untenured professor.

It is also important to keep in mind that some tenured professors will still not be willing to dissent or critically question the administration or leadership. Maybe a professor has two grants that she gets course releases to administer, and the support from the university is critical to their success. In her mind, it is not a wise decision to cross the administration. On the other hand, some tenured professors may speak out at every opportunity. Now that there is some comfort in their position, they feel the need to criticize all decisions and changes. Neither of these will serve the change process; it is necessary to support both in positive ways and to encourage a voice that will help lead change.

Power

Without a doubt, the tenured faculty members have power, and the full professor has the most. These faculty members have put in the time and effort to attain the highest level of an academic. Administrations will listen to them because in some instances this group of faculty members will outlast many deans and presidents.

This group has immense power when its members come together as a collective. Deans can be removed and presidents can get votes of no confidence. If this group can make changes like that to the college and university, imagine what it could do for programs and students.

Individually, these professors have power as well. They have built careers and spent time at conferences and meetings, meeting other leaders in their fields. The connections can lead to grant information and calls, leads on projects needing support in the nation, and leadership opportunities that benefit the programs, colleges, and universities. For example, a full professor may have a seat on a state committee looking at field experiences for preservice teachers. Through that work, he meets a representative looking for a school and university to field test a new observation measure. The relationship works to help grow the program, the professor, and the profession.

MOVING FORWARD

To move forward with educational reform, this group needs to be addressed. This may be the single most influential group of professionals in the education arena that can bring about change. In order to do so, education programs must connect the tenured faculty with new faculty in nontraditional ways. The tenured faculty also needs to have connections to the public schools in challenging ways. Finally, the tenured professor must also have continuous professional development that is meaningful and appropriate.

Connect with New Faculty

In a previous chapter, the idea was to connect new faculty with veteran faculty in an effort to guide and mentor the new faculty members. For this perspective, the idea is to connect the veteran faculty with new faculty in order to share insights and views of schooling. The collaboration between the junior faculty and the veteran faculty is critical to the success of educational reform.

Creating opportunities for collaboration is not about mentoring in a sense that one group is teaching the other group. Both of these groups have important ideas and information to bring to the table for discussion as a basis of educational reform. The obstacle has been that the groups tend to have rigid hierarchical ideas about each other. Condensing behaviors from tenured faculty to untenured faculty can happen in any institution. Other badges of elitism include snobbery about degrees, a PhD versus an EdD versus a master's, or where the degrees were granted. When faculty members form cliques with each other based on the degree or the alma mater, there is no chance for collaboration to improve schools.

Therefore, chairs, deans, and leaders in teacher education need to create meaningful opportunities for all groups to work together. The first step is getting the faculty to think of themselves as a faculty and not as junior and tenured faculty. This really involves changing the culture of the academy; in some colleges it will be radical, while others are already there. Once the faculty members start working as a team, other stakeholders need to be brought in, including public school teachers, parents, and administrators.

Connection to Schools

Tenured faculty members need to be reconnected to the public school system. The trend seems to be that the longer a professor is in the profession, the further away from the reality of the daily classroom he gets. Full professors are teaching doctoral candidates (which is important, as previously discussed) who do not have a defined connection to public schools. If the full professor is the apex of the academic mind, then that mind needs to be put to work solving the problems that are facing our schools, and that cannot be done without time and attention to the classroom.

Traditional roles of university relationships may not work for the tenured professor. Most programs require clinical supervision for the preservice teachers; this may not be the kind of connection the tenured professor needs in order to help. Educator preparation programs need to create roles for all types of professors to play in the relationships with public schools. Some of these roles may not have existed before now. What if a tenured professor with expertise in diversity worked as the parent liaison for a campus? Or a former principal who is a professor served as an educational law resource for new teachers? The possibilities of meaningful partnerships are endless, and it is imperative to begin creating them.

Continual Professional Development

Many colleges and universities hold lifelong learning as a value for their programs and students, but it seems by the time an academic becomes tenured, the time for continued learning is gone. Universities encourage professional development for instructor and new faculty members but rarely address the needs of the tenured professor. Even in faculty development efforts, the focus is primarily on the new or inexperienced faculty member. This group has professional development needs, too.

Challenges to professional development for the tenured professor are many. Time is a limited commodity and highly protected. The variety of needs is great as well as the challenge of gaining buy-in from the faculty. Tenured faculty members could be brought on board by understanding the needs for lifelong learning and the connection to educational reform. Unless we are constantly thinking about change and the possibilities of the future and the attempts of the past, then there will be no headway. Refresher courses could be offered as brown-bag workshops on the change process or legislation facing higher education. As long as the topics are meaningful and relevant, the tenured faculty can learn some things to help change education for the better.

CONCLUSIONS

All in all, the tenured professor is the most challenging perspective for educational reform. These professors are a unique group that can affect teacher preparation not only through the initial preparation program but also the doctoral programs in education. Tenured professors have the challenge to overcome their own expertise in order make changes. On the other hand, the tenured professor has more power than any other perspective to make change. By bringing this group on board, real educational reform is possible.

REFERENCE

Sarason, S. B. (1996). *Revisiting "The Culture of the School and the Problem of Change."* New York: Teachers College Press.

Chapter Eight

A Call to Action

The purpose of this text is to connect the varied perspectives in teacher education to the challenges facing the profession for educational reform. Oftentimes a specific group is targeted for an innovation or reform and the implications or ramifications for other professional groups are overlooked. By compartmentalizing reform movements in education, innovations may take hold in one perspective but not be wholly adopted or recognized by the entire teacher education community. In order for any reform movement or positive change to occur in American education, the profession needs to recognize the challenges and obstacles unique to each perspective invested in the educational system.

Each of these perspectives has unique and varied challenges and obstacles and calls for a gamut of strategies to optimize its role in educational reform. However, there are several major strategies that encompass all the perspectives needed for successful educational reform. The five major issues that relate to all perspectives are: mentoring, connection to schools and universities, unique strengths, accountability, and collaboration.

Mentoring

Each of the perspectives of education can benefit from well-developed, sustained mentoring. Many of the mentoring programs that are in effect currently are traditional mentoring programs. Typically, a new teacher or professor is assigned a more experienced teacher or professor to guide her through the first years in her new profession. Many of these mentor partnerships are partnerships in name only; a very superficial relationship is the only outcome. By forcing a mentorship pairing, the very essence of the relationship is undermined. New approaches to mentoring need to be investigated.

Mentoring for new teachers and professors could be very similar. The first few years in each profession are critical. New classroom teachers need sustained support to acclimate to the culture and climate of their school and campus. Adjusting to the demands of classrooms filled with children from all backgrounds and abilities is a process that takes months and even years. Having a relationship with a veteran teacher can help transition the preservice teacher into the role of teacher. Partnership with other new teachers can also help the process of acclimation. Discussing issues and ideas with someone who is also experiencing the same things can foster support and cognitive growth. The same ideas apply to the new professor. A tenured faculty member mentors the assistant professor through the navigation of the systems of service, teaching, and scholarship, but a relationship with another assistant professor can also support the faculty member in his year or years of transition.

Mentoring is also needed for the veteran teachers and the tenured faculty. As a teacher or professor grows in her career, new responsibilities are added and new challenges arise. It would be beneficial for veteran educators to have the opportunity to draw on the experiences of peers who have faced the same challenges. For example, a newly tenured faculty member may be asked to mentor a new assistant professor. The only experience in mentoring the tenured faculty member has is that of being mentored. By connecting faculty members and teachers through a mentoring network, a helping hand and shoulder for support are always available.

Additionally, educators need to stop thinking about mentoring as finite and restricted. Many times the new teacher has an assigned mentor for the first year. What happens when that teacher also has concerns in future years? That new teacher is assigned to the teacher across the hall. Maybe their personalities do not mesh; maybe the mentor has other stressors that year. What if the assigned mentor does not meet the needs of the new teacher? Mentoring should involve a network of educators who support each other whether the teachers and faculty are experienced or inexperienced, formally assigned or not. The education professors must make mentoring each other a professional standard if changes are going to be made.

Connection to Schools and Universities

The next major change in educational organizations is the connection to schools and universities. The partnership between the public schools and the colleges and universities of education is vital to the success of teacher preparation programs. Universities cannot prepare teachers without the input of the public school community, and schools need the support of colleges and universities to help professional development stay current in educational research, among other things. The relationship is symbiotic; neither can survive without the other. Yet many times both try to function independently, with little or no regard for the needs or possible contributions of the other. In order to fully engage in educational reform, both entities need to understand the necessity for each other and begin to move toward more times for connecting.

Opportunities for working with schools and universities should be available to all educators. Obviously, classroom teachers need to be utilized as mentors and supervisors for preservice teachers, but that is not the only way their talents should be used. Classroom teachers should be offering their expertise on advisory councils for university programs. They should be offering professional development for university faculty. They should be coteaching with university professors in the teacher preparation programs. New teachers need to be connected to the university through cosponsored induction programs that support them the first years.

All university faculty should be connected with a public school in some way. Traditionally, university faculty members have worked with public schools in placing and observing student teachers. For the education world to improve, the professors need to be engaged with the schools in new and innovative ways. University content professors could coteach in the high schools. They should be active on advisory boards for the schools. They should be offering professional development. They should be in the classrooms asking questions about the needs of the teachers.

Too often these connections are limited in scope or personnel. One staff member may be in charge of all of the field placements for a program, and no professors set foot in the schools. Programs in which the university faculty and the public school teachers do not know each other cannot move toward more innovative and effective teacher preparation programs. By creating connections and opportunities to interact, relationships will develop. Connections are the first step in making collaboration possible.

Collaboration

The definition of collaboration is working together. In education, the various perspectives oftentimes work independently toward resolution of a common issue. In order for the profession to grow and become effective for all children, universities, colleges, and schools need to work together to solve the problems at hand. The difference between connections and collaboration is that educators who have connections may share information, but they go back to their respective institutions to work. Collaboration means that the professionals share information and then use those conversations to inform new ways to address the problems.

Examples of collaboration include action research that is conducted by teams of teachers and professors, curriculum development undertaken by teams of professionals, and grant writing and implementation between school and university faculties. The possibilities for collaboration are endless, yet right now most of the collaborative events in schools and universities are loosely defined and finite. The cultural shift that needs to happen is that when facing an issue or problem, the school or university does not consider addressing it without the input and support of the other. Collaboration between the public schools and the institutions of higher education must become an automatic response rather than an afterthought when facing a challenge.

Unique Strengths

Each of the perspectives previously discussed has unique strengths and challenges. For educational reform to happen, each of the perspectives needs to utilize and be called on to offer their strengths to the movement. As people move through the different stages of their professional growth, they will add new skills to their repertoires and also find new insights related to the new professional experiences. The new stage only enhances the prior experiences, and all these together create the unique strengths of the perspectives.

The preservice teachers provide a connection between the university and the classroom, bringing new approaches and strategies to the classroom teachers. New classroom teachers have the foundation of their educator preparation programs behind them as well as an unending supply of idealism and creativity. Veteran classroom teachers have the wisdom of years of experience and the understanding of the educational system. Each of these groups of teachers is ready to be called on to help make changes that will benefit the children who are in the public schools.

The graduate students in education are also idealistic and eager to implement new strategies and approaches to instruction and curriculum. As the members of this group become the new assistant professors of the academy, they bring their eagerness and expertise to the teacher preparation programs. As they continue on to become tenured professors, they gain the experience of working in the academy and the wisdom of years working and researching in education. Again, this group should be willing to help serve the needs of the children of the United States at any time.

Each of the perspectives was discussed in detail previously. What is important to understand in this final chapter is that educators must trust each vital group as professionals. In the realm of professional educators, there is a tendency to belittle the perspective of another or different stakeholder. The university professor may think the classroom teacher is happy handing out worksheets and having students read aloud from the book while classroom teachers may think the university professor is an aloof, condescending know-it-all. And both of those groups will almost always overlook the new or preservice groups as having any potential contributions to the effort. All groups have something to give, and all groups are needed for there to be any significant change in the way education happens in the United States.

Accountability

With No Child Left Behind (2001), accountability became a high-stakes game for teachers and students in the public schools. A decade later, high-stakes accountability is moving into teacher education with value-added metrics and impact on student achievement. The requirements are the same for public school teachers. NCLB asks for data that shows the direct effect of a teacher on student achievement. Texas is answering that, like many other states, with new content exams in each content area in high school (STAAR).

In teacher education, the call has been made for programs to provide evidence that their candidates have an impact on student learning. Again, Texas, like many states, has developed and implemented value-added metrics that evaluate the effect of a teacher education program on student achievement. Accountability in education is not going away, and if the system is to continue, all educators must step up to help change the way the system works.

The new culture of accountability only increases the need for all the professional educators and future professional educators to work together and form a powerful voice in the United States. The issues of the quality of public schools and universities cannot be separated. The teachers in the public schools are graduates of the university preparation programs. Their professors were graduates of the public schools. The children and adolescents in the classrooms are the future teachers and professors. What affects one of the institutions will affect all the institutions. Educators must come together to take responsibility and make the necessary changes to ensure the public schools as well as the colleges and universities are effective and continue to be effective.

The options that are looming in the horizon for both the public schools and the universities are not in the best interests of either institution. Privatization of public schools is not an answer that is in the best interests of the children or the teachers. Business models of practice are not effective for education. Capitalization and competition will not make sure the young poor student gets an education and chances for success. If the educators in the United States do not come together to offer plans of improvement, then plans will be made without their input.

CONCLUDING THOUGHTS

The time has come for American educators to pull together to make a change in the education system. Disjointed and disconnected efforts have proved not

only divisive but also detrimental to the overall culture of education today.
No perspective or group can be left out of educational reform. All groups
must take responsibility for the state of the system today. Good things are
happening in places; ineffective things are happening elsewhere. The university professor who prepares preservice teachers can no longer worry only
about her graduates but must also consider others in the system. The same is
true for classroom teachers. One effective teacher cannot turn away from the
needs of the whole system just because his students are being well prepared.
It will take everyone to forge a new direction in education.

The collaborative call to action is important today. The federal government and the state legislations are becoming more and more active in education by enacting legislation that dictates standards, assessment, and accountability measures. If the professional educators of today do not stand together
and answer the needs of the system, the teachers of tomorrow will be teaching in the system developed and implemented by the lawmakers. It is up to
us.